Daily *warm-ups*

WORLD CULTURES

Kate O'Halloran

WALCH PUBLISHING

The classroom teacher may reproduce materials in this book for classroom use only.
The reproduction of any part for an entire school or school system is strictly prohibited.
No part of this publication may be transmitted, stored, or recorded in any form
without written permission from the publisher.

1   2   3   4   5   6   7   8   9   10

ISBN 0-8251-5082-5

Copyright © 2004
Walch Publishing
P. O. Box 658 • Portland, Maine 04104-0658
walch.com
Printed in the United States of America

SUSTAINABLE FORESTRY INITIATIVE

Certified Chain of Custody
Promoting Sustainable
Forest Management
www.sfiprogram.org

SGS-SFI/COC-US09/5501

Table of Contents

iii

Introduction . . . . *v*

The Meaning of Culture. 1–11

North Africa and Southwest Asia 12–35

Sub-Saharan Africa 36–53

South Asia 54–70

Southeast Asia 71–84

Australia and Oceania 85–96

East Asia 97–119

Northern Eurasia and Central Asia 120–135

Europe 136–152

Latin America and the Caribbean 153–166

The United States and Canada 167–180

Answer Key 181

The *Daily Warm-Ups* series is a wonderful way to turn extra classroom minutes into valuable learning time. The 180 quick activities—one for each day of the school year—present and review information about different cultures of the world. These daily activities may be used at the very beginning of class to get students into learning mode, near the end of class to make good educational use of that transitional time, in the middle of class to shift gears between lessons—or whenever else you have minutes that now go unused. In addition to providing students with fascinating information, they are a natural path to other classroom activities involving critical thinking.

Daily Warm-Ups are easy-to-use reproducibles—simply photocopy the day's activity and distribute it. Or make a transparency of the activity and project it on the board. You may want to use the activities for extra-credit points or as a check on the knowledge and critical-thinking skills that are acquired over time.

These activities have been chosen to address more of the "human" aspects of world cultures, focusing less on politics, war, and conflict. Some of the topics in the activities may be less familiar to students. In such cases, you may want to encourage students to use their textbooks or other resources to complete the activity.

The first section of this book looks at the features that contribute to cultures. You may want to use these activities to make students aware of these aspects of culture. The rest of the book is organized by region. Within each region, activities address certain key topics. To help you choose activities by topic, each activity title includes an icon. Here is a key to the topics:

transmission of culture—proverbs, myths, customs, etc.

keeping time—calendars, festivals, days of remembrance

contributions to world culture—religion, food, cultural heritage sites, etc.

language and literature

important historical events

people of note

the arts

how physical geography affects culture

cultures in contact, in conflict, and in the process of change

However you choose to use them, *Daily Warm-Ups* are a convenient and useful supplement to your regular lesson plans. Make every minute of your class time count!

⬈ Proverbs and Daily Life

Proverbs are short sayings people use all the time. Some proverbs give practical advice, such as "Look before you leap." Some encourage people dealing with problems: "It's darkest just before dawn." And some pass judgment on a person's actions: "More haste, less speed."

The same thing holds true for cultures all around the world. All kinds of different peoples use proverbs. They are a way of passing on information within a culture. Through proverbs, people learn what is considered moral behavior.

Think of a proverb you are familiar with. (If you can't think of any, use one of the ones above.) What is the purpose of the proverb—to give advice or encouragement, to pass judgment, or something else? Does it reflect a certain type of culture? Write one or two sentences for your answer.

1

❀ A Variety of Calendars

What year is it? How do you know?

We take time for granted, but accurate clocks and calendars are fairly recent developments. And the Gregorian calendar—the calendar used in the United States—isn't the only one used in the world. In fact, about forty different calendars are in use today! However, most of them are used primarily to determine religious dates. Most countries use the Gregorian calendar for official activities.

The Gregorian calendar is based on a solar year, which is 365.242 days. That is how long it takes the earth to travel around the sun.

2

In the Gregorian calendar, a year has 365 ¼ days. But a day is a 24-hour period. How can a calendar adjust for a quarter of a day? Write one or two sentences for your answer.

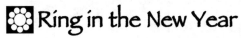

✿ Ring in the New Year

In the United States, we celebrate the start of a new year on January 1. The word *January* comes from the Roman god Janus. In Roman religion, Janus was the god of beginnings. Janus had two faces, one looking forward and one looking backward. In January we look back at the old year and look ahead at the new one.

However, the ancient Romans didn't always celebrate the new year in January. For a long time, their new-year celebration was in late March, at the start of spring. This is the time when new crops are planted and the whole earth seems to make a fresh start. Over time, different emperors made changes to the Roman calendar. The calendar and the seasons ended up out of sync. Finally, Julius Caesar set up a new calendar. He declared that the year began on January 1.

Because of that Roman calendar, many countries now celebrate the new year on January 1. But many other cultures celebrate the new year at different times. What do you know about different ways people celebrate the new year? Write down as many as you can think of. Include your own new-year's traditions and symbols.

3

⊕ Influential Development

Some developments are minor conveniences. Some change the world. We can learn how important a development is by asking a few questions. What is its effect on society? Does it improve people's quality of life? How many people benefit from it?

Here are some developments made in the past 150 years. Use the questions given above to assess them. Which of these developments would you consider the most important? Write one or two sentences to explain your answer.

Internal combustion engine
- makes it easier to travel long distances and to transport goods
- most available in United States, Europe; least available in India, China

Water purification and sanitation (toilets)
- reduces death from dysentery, cholera, etc.
- most available in industrialized nations

Generation and transmission of electricity
- led to practical inventions, including lighting, refrigeration, radio, television, computers, the Internet
- most available in industrialized nations

4

🌐 World Heritage Sites

UNESCO is part of the United Nations. The name stands for "United Nations Educational, Scientific, and Cultural Organization." One of its programs is the World Heritage Convention. More than 150 nations have joined. Members can suggest sites for the World Heritage List. This is a list of places around the world that are important to everyone, not just to one country. To be included, a site must have either cultural or natural importance. Sites can be natural or made by humans. The important thing is that a site must have outstanding universal value.

More than 730 places have been listed as World Heritage Sites, in more than 125 countries. Some of them are not very well known. Some are famous.

Think about the criteria for being listed. The site must have universal value and either cultural or natural importance. What places, in the United States and around the world, can you think of that should be World Heritage Sites? List as many places as you can that meet the criteria.

5

Languages and Loanwords

Whenever two languages are in contact with each other for a long time, they influence each other. The most obvious influence is in vocabulary. When one culture has no word for something that comes from a different place, it often adopts the other place's word. Such words are called loanwords. For example, basketball was invented in the United States. When other countries adopted the game, they needed a word for it, too. The easiest thing was to adopt the word *basketball* along with the game. But, of course, the word needed to be adapted to fit into different languages. In French it became *le basket*. In Japanese, it's *basuke*. Turks play *basketbol*.

Some languages easily adopt loanwords from other languages. But some cultures resist adding foreign words. They try to develop their own terms for new ideas.

Which approach to loanwords do you think is best for a language, easy adoption or the resistance of foreign words? Write one or two sentences to explain your answer.

6

☀ History: Cause and Effect

In many ways, history is a long, long chain of cause and effect. Because a storm sank the Mongol fleet in 1274, the Mongols did not conquer Japan. Because an Italian sailor was stubborn, Europe and the Americas came into contact in 1492. Because of a German mapmaker, America was named for a later explorer, not Christopher Columbus.

Think of at least four events that changed history. Name each one, and write one or two sentences explaining why it is important.

7

Living National Treasures

For centuries, Japanese culture was separate from the rest of the world. Then, after 1853, Japan came into contact with other cultures. People began to replace old ways with new approaches. Many Japanese traditions began to disappear.

The Japanese government saw these traditions as important. They wanted to save their heritage. In 1950, the government created a special honor for traditional artists: "Living National Treasure." This title is given to artists who meet certain standards. They must be outstanding in their field. Their products must be used in everyday life. And they must use time-honored techniques. People who have received this honor include potters, musicians, and actors.

8

Now, other countries are also starting to recognize their Living National Treasures. What criteria would you use to identify Living National Treasures in this country? Make a list of criteria. Be as detailed as you can. Then name several people who would fit your definition of Living National Treasure.

🎵 The Arts

Human beings have always had the urge to create art. Even before written history, people expressed themselves in painting and sculpture. They probably also expressed themselves in other ways, such as through music, dance, and theater.

The same thing is true of cultures around the world today. All cultures develop their own ways of expressing themselves through the arts. People may decorate their bodies in a distinctive way. They may have a special puppet theater, or musical instruments, or dance styles.

Each item listed below is an art form that developed in one culture. The country it comes from is given in parentheses. Write **D** for dance and music or **T** for theater and puppetry on the line beside each one.

_____1. Bunraku (Japan)

_____2. ch'angguk (Korea)

_____3. commedia dell'arte (Italy)

_____4. fado (Portugal)

_____5. flamenco (Spain)

_____6. hula (Hawaii)

_____ 7. merengue (Dominican Republic)

_____ 8. Noh (Japan)

_____ 9. raga (India)

_____10. jazz (United States)

_____11. tango (Argentina)

_____12. wayang kulit (Indonesia)

9

Geography and Human Culture

Think about the world. What one place on the entire planet is best suited for people to live? The answer is . . . nowhere. Every place has advantages and disadvantages. One place may have a great climate but be subject to earthquakes and hurricanes. Another may be safe from storms but have a large number of disease-carrying insects. Other places may be too wet, too dry, too cold, or too hot.

But people live in all these places. People live in the extreme north, where the temperature is below freezing for nine months of the year. They live in the Gobi Desert, where less than 10 cm (4 in) of rain falls every year and temperatures range from –40°C to 45°C. And they live in all the hot, cold, wet, dry, storm-swept regions in between.

10

In order to live in all these places, people have to adapt. They develop clothes, tools, housing, and lifestyles that fit the environment. They also change the environment. For example, in areas with low rainfall, water from rivers may be used to irrigate fields.

Think of all the ways you know of that people adapt themselves to their environment, and how they adapt the environment to themselves. List as many as you can.

🎎 Learning About Culture

The culture of a nation—any nation—is built up over time. It is shaped by many things, including physical environment and the events of history. Eventually, a unique culture develops. Many cultures have things in common. But they also have differences.

We learn the customs of our culture unconsciously, as children. We learn how to greet people, what different gestures mean, how to eat. But people who visit a different country often find they don't understand the subtle rules of the culture. This can leave them feeling uncomfortable.

Imagine that you are making a long visit to a country with a culture very different from yours. Meals include unfamiliar foods. They are eaten with different utensils. Even though you speak the language, you often misunderstand things. You're sure you will figure it out eventually. But right now, you keep embarrassing yourself!

What could you do to make this adjustment period easier? What attitudes will probably be most helpful? Write down as many helpful attitudes and approaches as you can think of.

11

⬢ Arabic Proverbs

These proverbs are heard in Arabic-speaking nations. Like many proverbs, they have both a literal meaning and a hidden one. Each one would be used in certain situations but not in others.

Read each proverb carefully to find its hidden meaning. Then match each proverb with the situations where it might be used.

Proverbs

_____ 1. If speech is silver, silence is gold.

_____ 2. Safety is in slowness; regret is in haste.

_____ 3. I believe what you say; I'm surprised at what you do.

_____ 4. They couldn't beat the donkey, so they beat the saddle.

_____ 5. The camel went through labor only to give birth to a mouse.

Situations

a. After a lot of effort, you get a small reward.

b. A person says one thing but does another.

c. One person says bad things about another.

d. Someone is rushing to finish a job.

e. The wrong person is blamed for something.

12

⛰ Saudi Arabia: Traditional Dress

Saudi Arabia is a hot, dry land. In earlier times, many of the people who lived there were nomads. They developed a way of dressing to suit their climate.

These clothes are still worn by most people in Saudi Arabia today. Both men and women keep their heads covered. They wear long, loose robes. These robes are warm in winter. They stop the body's moisture from evaporating in summer. Traditional clothes also meet the Islamic rule to dress modestly.

The names of these traditional garments are given in the box. Match each name with its description below.

a. abaaya	b. ghutra	c. shayla	d. thobe

_____ 1. scarf of black, gauzy fabric worn to cover a woman's face

_____ 2. long, black outer cloak that drapes a woman from head to ankle

_____ 3. man's long white robe, made in cotton or light wool

_____ 4. man's head covering, usually either white or red-and-white checks

13

☀ The Islamic Calendar

The calendar used in the United States is a solar calendar. It is based on how long it takes the earth to travel around the sun, or 365.24 days. The Islamic calendar is a lunar calendar. It has twelve months based on the motion of the moon. A lunar month is 29.53 days long. This means that the Islamic year is 354.36 days.

In the Islamic calendar, years are counted from the Hegira, or Muhammad's flight to Mecca. This happened in 622 C.E. So 622 C.E. is year 1 A.H. (Anno Hegira, year after the Hegira).

However, 1622 C.E. wasn't 1001 A.H. It was 1,031 A.H. In the Gregorian calendar, 1,000 years had passed, but 1,031 years had passed in the Islamic calendar. In 2022 C.E., the Gregorian calendar will have marked 1,400 years since the Hegira. In the Islamic calendar, it will be the year 1443 A.H.—1,442 years since the Hegira.

Why do you think the years in these two calendars don't match? Write one or two sentences to explain your answer.

❁ No Ruz: Iranian New Year

Iran's new-year festival is called No Ruz, or "new day." It has been celebrated for 3,000 years. The thirteen-day festival starts on March 20 or 21, after the spring equinox. In preparation, people clean their homes and make new clothes. They germinate wheat seeds as a symbol of renewal. Troubadours known as Haji Firuz parade through the streets to announce the new year. Each family sets up a ceremonial table, the *haft seen*. Each of the seven dishes on the table begins with the letter *s* in Farsi, the language of Iran. The dishes symbolize rebirth, health, happiness, prosperity, joy, patience, and beauty.

On the last Tuesday of the old year, families light small bonfires. They take turns jumping over the fire to get rid of illness and bad luck. Later in the evening children dress up and visit neighbors, banging on a metal bowl. The neighbors put treats in the visitors' bowls.

The first few days of No Ruz are spent visiting family and friends. Most people spend the last day of the festival outdoors. At the end of the day, the *sabzeh*, or sprouted wheat, is thrown away. Tradition says that the *sabzeh* has collected all the bad luck and worries of the past. The new year begins with a clean slate on the fourteenth of the month.

15

Many of the traditions of No Ruz are symbolic. What symbols are associated with your new-year celebration? Write down as many as you can.

🌐 Jerusalem, Holy City

Three of the world's major faiths began in Southwest Asia: Islam, Judaism, and Christianity. All three of these religions consider Jerusalem, the capital of Israel, one of their holy cities.

Write two or three sentences to explain what makes Jerusalem holy to each of these religions.

16

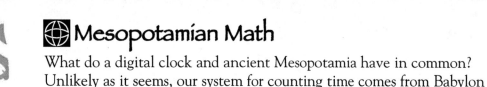

🌐 Mesopotamian Math

What do a digital clock and ancient Mesopotamia have in common? Unlikely as it seems, our system for counting time comes from Babylon of about 5,000 years ago.

The Babylonian system of math is one of the oldest in the world. While our counting system is based on 10, theirs was based on 60. They worked out a system of time based on 60: 60 seconds in a minute, 60 minutes in an hour.

Of course, back then, an hour could be longer or shorter, depending on the season. The Babylonians divided the time between sunrise and sunset by 12. Each ¹⁄₁₂ was one hour. In summer, when the sun rises earlier and sets later, the total time of daylight was longer. That meant the Babylonians were dividing a larger number by 12, so they had a long hour. In winter, of course, there was less daylight. An hour in winter was shorter. Only when mechanical clocks were invented did hours become a fixed length.

In the thousands of years since the fall of Babylon, their system of math has been replaced by our decimal system, a system based on multiples of 10 (10, 100, 1000, . . .). But one other element of Babylonian math is still in use today. It uses the number 360, which is 6 × 60. Can you name something that is divided into 360 degrees? (Hint: It's used a lot in geometry and astronomy. You use a protractor to measure it.)

17

⊕ Turkey: What Is It?

Most countries have landmarks. They can be buildings or natural features. They are sites that people around the world identify with that country.

This is a description of a Turkish landmark. Read the description. Then name the landmark being described.

Built on the site of an earlier church, it was completed in 537 C.E. as a Christian church. Its name means "Holy Wisdom."

In 1453, the Turks conquered Constantinople. The church became a mosque. Over the years, the Christian symbols and mosaics were covered by plaster, as Islamic code forbids representations of people. Other architectural changes were also made, including the addition of four slender minarets, or towers, at its outer corners.

In 1935, it was converted into a museum.

What is it?

18

🌐 Egypt: What Is It?

Most countries have landmarks. They can be buildings or natural features. They are sites that people around the world identify with that country.

This is a description of an Egyptian landmark. Read the description. Then name the landmark being described.

Carved from a single block of limestone about 4,600 years ago, this strange sculpture rises 20 m (66 ft) from the Sahara Desert. Some 60 m (240 ft) long, it has the body of a lion and the head of a man. It has often been buried by the shifting sands of the desert. The windblown sand has eroded the soft stone, wearing away the details of the sculpture. It still remains one of the wonders of the world.

What is it?

19

World Heritage Sites: Turkey

Nine sites in Turkey have been named World Heritage Sites by UNESCO. Four of them are described below. Read the descriptions. Then write one or two sentences to explain why you think each site is on the list. Use anything else you know about the sites in your explanation.

Historic Areas of Istanbul
Associated with political, religious, and artistic events for over 2,000 years, important sites in Istanbul include the Hagia Sophia and the Süleymaniye Mosque.

Göreme National Park and the Rock Sites of Cappadocia
The volcanic rock in this area has been worn into strange shapes. Underground towns and fine examples of Byzantine art on rock sanctuary walls are among the sights here.

Hierapolis-Pamukkale
The mineral forests and petrified waterfalls of this eerie landscape were formed by calcite-laden water. The ruins of a 2,000-year-old thermal spa can still be seen.

Archaeological Site of Troy
The siege of Troy in the thirteenth century B.C.E. was immortalized by Homer in *The Iliad*. Excavations began here in 1870, and work at the site continues today.

20

 Arabic English

How much Arabic do you speak? You might be surprised. A lot of English words have been borrowed from Arabic. Read the following passage. Circle all the words that were originally Arabic.

As I sat on the scarlet mohair sofa, eating apricots and oranges, I found myself thinking about an algebra problem I'd seen in a magazine. I tried to work it out, but the only answer I could get was zero.

21

Mulla Nasrudin

Throughout Southwest Asia, people tell stories about Mulla Nasrudin. In some stories he is very clever; in some he is a fool. But in all the stories, he has his own way of looking at things.

These stories are part of the Sufi tradition. Sufism is a form of Islam that stresses spirituality. Sufi stories teach people to recognize rigid thinking patterns.

Here are two stories about Mulla Nasrudin.

A friend asked Nasrudin, "How old are you?"

"Fifty."

"What? Mulla, you told me the same thing five years ago!"

"You see?" the Mulla replied. "I never go back on my word."

While cutting the Mulla's hair, the barber said, "How funny—your hair is almost white, but your beard has no silver in it!"

"There's nothing funny about it," said the Mulla. "My hair is twenty years older than my beard!"

Why do you think stories like this are used as teaching exercises? Write two or three sentences to explain your answer.

 Persian Loanwords

Persian, also known as Farsi, is spoken widely in Iran and Afghanistan. Some Farsi speakers also live in other Persian Gulf countries, including Iraq, Oman, and Bahrain. And, of course, you speak some Farsi—although you may not know it.

The following scrambled words came to English from Farsi. Unscramble them to find some common English words.

1. aaabzr   _____

2. pinsach   _____

3. ecchk   _____

4. giacm   _____

5. haikk   _____

23

 Naguib Mahfouz

Writer Naguib Mahfouz won the 1988 Nobel Prize for literature. Mahfouz sets many of his novels, short stories, and plays in Cairo. But while the setting is Egypt, the themes of Mahfouz's work are universal: reason versus faith, love, the nature of time.

Read the quotations from Mahfouz below. Choose one of them. Then write two or three sentences explaining what you think he means.

"You can tell whether a man is clever by his answers. You can tell whether a man is wise by his questions."

"The real malady is fear of life, not death."

"Literature should be more revolutionary than revolutions themselves; . . . writers must find the means to continue to be critical of the negative elements in the sociopolitical reality."

"Freedom of expression must be considered sacred, and thought can only be corrected by counter thought."

24

☀ The Rosetta Stone

In 1798, Napoleon Bonaparte invaded Egypt. The next year, French soldiers in Egypt found a slab of stone near the village of Rosetta.

This stone, which is about three feet high, turned out to be very important. Write two or three sentences explaining the importance of the Rosetta Stone.

25

 Camp David Accords

In September 1978, Anwar el-Sadat of Egypt and Menachem Begin of Israel met with U.S. President Jimmy Carter at Camp David. After twelve days of negotiations, they signed two agreements. One was to put an end to fighting between Egypt and Israel. The other defined future relations between the two countries.

In discussing these meetings, Menachem Begin said, "It is much more difficult to show civil courage than military courage."

What do you think Begin meant by this? Write one or two sentences explaining your answer.

26

🌀 Key Figures in the Middle East

The people named below have all played important roles in the Middle East. Match each person with his or her country or organization listed in the box.

Egypt Israel Jordan PLO (Palestine Liberation Organization) Syria

1. Yasir Arafat _____

2. Hafez al-Asad _____

3. Menachem Begin _____

4. David Ben-Gurion _____

5. Hussein bin Talal _____

6. Golda Meir _____

7. Hosni Mubarak_____

8. Gamal Abdel Nasser _____

9. Yitzhak Rabin _____

10. Anwar el-Sadat _____

27

Decoration in Islamic Architecture

Islamic architecture varies widely from country to country. It is affected by local traditions, climate, building materials, and so on. But one element unifies all these different styles: surface decoration. Walls, floors, and ceilings are often patterned. The pattern may be inlaid in stone, carved, painted, or tiled. Some designs are clearly based on geometry. Some incorporate calligraphy, or decorative writing. Some use floral motifs. They often interlace and use varying colors and textures to create a sense of depth and movement.

However, images of people and animals are rarely used in this type of decoration. They are never found on buildings used for religious purposes. Based on what you know about Islam, write one or two sentences explaining this.

28

 Arabic Calligraphy

"Calligraphy" means "beautiful writing." Much Islamic art is based on calligraphy. This is in part because the Arabic alphabet was used to copy the Koran. Muslims believe this holy book contains God's very words. Another reason is that Muslim tradition did not allow paintings of people to be used in mosques.

Islamic calligraphy developed into a fine art. The twenty-eight letters of the Arabic alphabet are written and read from right to left. A flowing, cursive style is often used. This makes the letters very decorative. However, beauty is not seen as more important than legibility. This means calligraphers must plan carefully before beginning to write.

عليكم السلام

This says "As-salamu alaykum," which means "peace be with you." It is used as a greeting in Arabic.

Try copying this calligraphy. You may draw it freehand or trace the lines. Start at the upper right-hand corner. The vertical strokes are made from top to bottom. The horizontal strokes are made from right to left.

29

🌐 Food in North Africa

Morocco, a country in North Africa, is famous for its food. The country is fortunate in both climate and setting. Many fruits and vegetables grow there, including oranges, lemons, dates, and olives. Seafood is plentiful along the coast. Lamb and poultry are raised inland. Imported spices are used to give food flavor.

Some popular Moroccan foods are named in the box. Write the name of each one beside its description.

bisteeya	couscous	harissa	tagine

30

_____ 1. spicy meat or chicken stew

_____ 2. fine grains of semolina, steamed over stew, served with stew on top

_____ 3. savory pie with layers of chicken, eggs, lemon-onion sauce, wrapped in thin pastry, topped with cinnamon and sugar

_____ 4. hot paste, usually served with couscous, made with chiles, garlic, cumin, coriander, mint, and oil

 Geography and Civilization

Two of the world's earliest civilizations developed in Southwest Asia and North Africa: Egypt and Mesopotamia. These two "cradles of civilization" were different in many ways, but they also had important similarities.

Think about the geography of these two places. Then name as many geographic similarities and differences as you can.

© 2004 Walch Publishing

◆ Bedouin in the UAR

Fifty years ago, the Bedouin of the United Arab Emirates were nomadic herders. They rode camels from camp to camp across the arid land. Then, in the 1960s, oil was found in the region. Today, most Bedouin live in permanent settlements. Instead of camels, they steer Land Rovers through the desert, cell phones in hand.

The Bedouin say that they have seen two eras in one lifetime. Their lives today are far more comfortable than before oil brought wealth to their country. Access to health care and education has increased. Still, some Bedouin feel that they have lost something by the change. One Bedouin poem goes:

> My tears leave a path in the night sand,
> For that which was dear to me has vanished.

What do you think the poet meant by these lines? Write two or three sentences explaining the poem.

32

 Governments in Southwest Asia

Listed below are the countries of Southwest Asia. Choose the correct government type from the box for each one. Then write the letter on the line beside each country.

a. democracy	d. republic	f. theocratic
b. federation	e. republic under	republic
c. monarchy	military regime	g. transitional

_____ 1. Afghanistan

_____ 2. Bahrain

_____ 3. Cyprus

_____ 4. Iran

_____ 5. Iraq

_____ 6. Israel

_____ 7. Jordan

_____ 8. Kuwait

_____ 9. Lebanon

_____ 10. Oman

_____ 11. Qatar

_____ 12. Saudi Arabia

_____ 13. Syria

_____ 14. Turkey

_____ 15. United Arab Emirates

_____ 16. Yemen

33

Last Names in Turkey

In Turkey today, people have a given name and a family name. For example, in the name Uktu Okcuoglu, Okcuoglu—which means "son of an archer"—is the family name. Uktu's parents, brothers, and sisters share the name Okcuoglu. His given name, Uktu, means "victory."

Before 1933, most Turks used only a given name. People lived in small villages, where everyone knew everyone else. Last names weren't really needed. As part of his effort to modernize Turkey, leader Mustafa Kemal Atatürk said that everyone must choose a family name. He was given the family name "Atatürk" by the Turkish General National Assembly. It means "father of the Turks."

Some people chose family names that had a special meaning to them. For example, one general took the name "Inönü." This was the site of a battle he had won. Some people took names that showed their occupations. Okcuoglu, or "son of an archer," is an example of this. Some just adopted the title "bey," which means "mister," as a family name.

34

Imagine that you have been ordered to adopt a new family name. Choose a name that has some meaning for you. Write two or three sentences explaining why you chose this name.

 Governments in North Africa

These are the countries of Africa north of the Sahara. Choose the correct government type from the box for each one. Then write the letter on the line beside each country name.

a. contested territory	b. republic	c. military	d. monarchy

_____ 1. Algeria

_____ 2. Egypt

_____ 3. Libya

_____ 4. Morocco

_____ 5. Tunisia

_____ 6. Western Sahara

35

⛰️ African Proverbs

The Yoruba of Nigeria have a saying: "A proverb is the horse that can carry one swiftly to the discovery of ideas." Different cultures often use proverbs to address the same values.

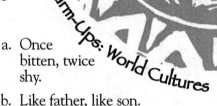

The ideas in these African proverbs are similar to proverbs heard in the United States. Match each numbered African proverb with the lettered American proverb that is closest to it in meaning.

___ 1. No matter how long a log may float in the water, it will never become a crocodile. (Gambia)

___ 2. You cannot pick up a pebble with one finger. (Malawi)

___ 3. If nothing touches the palm-leaves, they do not rustle. (Oji, Ashanti)

___ 4. A child who is to be successful is not to be reared exclusively on a bed of down. (Akan)

___ 5. The child of an elephant will not be a dwarf. (Yoruba)

___ 6. One who has been bitten by a snake lives in fear of worms. (Igbo)

a. Once bitten, twice shy.

b. Like father, like son.

c. Experience is the best teacher.

d. Many hands make light work.

e. There's no smoke without fire.

f. The leopard cannot change its spots.

36

© 2004 Walch Publishing

⛰ What's in a Name: Ghana

About 18 million people live in Ghana, a country in West Africa. Almost half of Ghanaians are members of the Akan tribe. In the Akan naming tradition, one of a baby's names is based on gender and the day of the week on which the baby is born. The table below shows the day-names for both boys and girls.

Day of the week	Male	Female
Sunday	Kwesi	Esi
Monday	Kwodwo	Adwoa
Tuesday	Kobena	Abena
Wednesday	Kweku	Ekua
Thursday	Yaw	Yaa
Friday	Kofi	Efua
Saturday	Kwame	Ama

37

If you had been named under this system, what would your name be? (If you don't know what day of the week you were born, figure out what day your birthday will be on this year. Use that day to determine your day-name.)

 Ethiopian Calendar

Around 330 C.E., many people in the African kingdom of Ethiopia converted to Christianity. Even today, almost 40 percent of the population is Christian. Ethiopia still uses the Julian Calendar, which most other countries stopped using in 1582.

The Julian calendar consists of thirteen months. Twelve months have thirty days each. The thirteenth month has five days, six days in a leap year. The year begins on the first day of the month of Meskerem. In the Gregorian calendar, this is September 11 (September 12 in a leap year). The last month is the short month.

The Ethiopian version of the calendar has one other unusual feature. It counts years differently from the Gregorian calendar. From September 11, when the new Ethiopian year starts, until December 31, when the Gregorian year ends, the two calendars are seven years apart. From January 1 to September 10, they are eight years apart. So when the Gregorian calendar said it was October 2000, the Ethiopian year was 1993.

According to the Ethiopian calendar, what year is it now? According to the Gregorian calendar, when will Ethiopia mark the start of the new millennium, 2000?

⊕ Olduvai Gorge

The Great Rift Valley is a gouge across eastern Africa. Caused by a shift in Earth's tectonic plates some 25 million years ago, it is more than 6,400 km (4,000 mi) long. At its widest, the valley is 80 km (50 mi) across. At its deepest, it is 1.6 km (1 mi) deep. One part of the rift is Olduvai Gorge, a 50-km- (30-mi) long gash in the Serengeti Plain. In 1911, a professor hunting butterflies there found some fossil bones. The bones interested archaeologists. Scientists began to excavate in the area, looking for information about early humans.

In 1959, Mary and Louis Leakey made an important discovery in Olduvai Gorge. They found a 1.8 million-year-old skull fragment.

Bone fragments from early hominids have been found in other parts of the world. Some recent finds come from hominids who lived almost 6 million years ago. Still, that early find at Olduvai Gorge was important. Why do you think this is? Write one or two sentences for your answer.

39

⊕ Ethiopia: What Is It?

Most countries have landmarks. They can be buildings or natural features. They are sites that people around the world identify with that country.

This is a description of an Ethiopian landmark. Read the description. Then name the landmark being described.

High in the mountains of Ethiopia, around 1250 C.E., these eleven buildings were carved from the volcanic rock they stand on. Some are almost completely hidden in deep stone trenches. Four are freestanding, attached to the surrounding rock only by their bases. All are connected by a maze of tunnels and passageways.

Possibly the oldest preserved architectural structures on the continent, they are still a site of pilgrimage for Coptic priests and lay worshippers.

What are they?

Saying "Hello" in Sierra Leone

Several languages are spoken in the West African nation of Sierra Leone. English is the official language, but it is only spoken by a few people. Mende is spoken mostly in the south. Temne is spoken in the north. Limba is spoken in the north-central region. Krio, an English-based Creole, is a first language for 10 percent of the population, but it is understood by 95 percent. Other languages include Kisi, Kono, Kuranko, Loko, Sherbro, and Susu.

Here are ways to say "hello" in five languages of Sierra Leone. Try saying each greeting. Then write one or two sentences explaining why so many languages are spoken in Sierra Leone.

Language	Greeting	Pronunciation
Fula	n'jallama	(en-JAH-lah-mah)
Krio	kusheyo	(koo-SHAY-o)
Limba	wali-wali	(WAHL ee WAHL ee)
Mende	ndiamo, biwa	(ndee-YAH-mo, BU-wah)
Temne	wan, sekke yo!	(wan, SEK-ay YO)

41

Anansi the Spider

In West Africa, people tell stories about Anansi the spider. He is a trickster, but often gets himself into trouble with his tricks. Anansi is cunning, but doesn't have much common sense.

The Anansi stories have spread to other parts of the world. In some countries, the trickster is a rabbit. In the southern United States, he is known as Brer Rabbit. In Venezuela, he's Tio Conejo—Uncle Rabbit. The rabbit is also known in many Caribbean countries.

Although the shape of the trickster may change, the stories often tell the same tale. Anansi the spider in Nigeria plays the same tricks as Brer Rabbit in the United States.

How do you think the Anansi stories spread to the Caribbean, Latin America, and the United States? Explain your answer in one or two clear sentences.

42

Pidgin English

In Nigeria, 400 different languages are spoken. Twelve of them are spoken by more than a million people. When Nigeria was a British colony, state schools taught English to Nigerian children.

Nigeria is no longer a colony. Still, the legacy of English remains. People combined English words with words from their own languages to form a new language, Pidgin English. Nigerians who don't know each other's languages can use Pidgin to communicate.

The Pidgin words in the box have been adapted from English words. Look at them carefully to identify the words they come from. Match each Pidgin word with its meaning. (Hint: If you get stuck, try sounding out the Pidgin words.)

abeg	adonkia	barawo	bifor-bifor	dorti-dorti
fren-fren	melesin	aipot	sawa	tineja

1. airport _____

2. favoritism _____

3. garbage _____

4. "I don't care" attitude _____

5. long ago _____

6. medicine _____

7. please _____

8. sour _____

9. teenager _____

10. thief _____

43

© 2004 Walch Publishing

☀ Ghana: Important Events

Here are some important events in Ghana's history. Number them in the order that they happened, from 1 to 11.

___ a. new democratic constitution introduced; Rawlings elected president

___ b. British proclaim coastal area crown colony

___ c. Nkrumah is overthrown in bloodless military coup

___ d. after two terms allowed by constitution, Rawlings's presidency ends

___ e. European colonial powers divide Africa; thousands of separate kingdoms become about 50 European colonies

___ f. Ghana becomes independent, with Kwame Nkrumah as prime minister

___ g. ethnic clashes within Ghana lead to many deaths

___ h. new laws abolish political parties, reduce civil rights; several coup attempts against Rawlings

___ i. first Europeans arrive in Ghana

___ j. reconciliation commission starts investigating human rights violations during military rule

___ k. succession of coups, governments; in 1981, Jerry Rawlings takes control

44

⊕ Desmond Tutu

Desmond Tutu was born in Transvaal, South Africa. He trained first as a teacher. Later he studied theology and became a priest. After several years teaching theology, he was appointed dean of St. Mary's Cathedral in Johannesburg. Tutu was the first black person to hold that position. In 1976 he became bishop of Lesotho. In 1978 he became the first black general secretary of the South African Council of Churches.

In all these positions, he spoke out for civil rights. He called for economic sanctions against South Africa to protest the policy of apartheid. In 1984 he was awarded the Nobel Peace Prize for his work.

In talking about apartheid, Tutu said, "We must not allow ourselves to become like the system we oppose. We cannot afford to use methods of which we will be ashamed when we look back, when we say, ' . . . we shouldn't have done that.' We must remember, my friends, that we have been given a wonderful cause. The cause of freedom! And you and I must be those who will walk with heads held high. We will say, 'We used methods that can stand the harsh scrutiny of history.'"

What do you think Bishop Tutu meant by this? Write one or two sentences explaining your answer.

45

© 2004 Walch Publishing

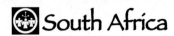 # South Africa

Here are some famous South Africans. Match each name with the correct description below.

___ 1. Christian Barnard   ___ 6. Nadine Gordimer

___ 2. Steve Biko   ___ 7. Miriam Makeba

___ 3. P. W. Botha   ___ 8. Nelson Mandela

___ 4. F. W. De Klerk   ___ 9. Charlize Theron

___ 5. Athol Fugard   ___ 10. Desmond Tutu

a. political prisoner; first postapartheid president; 1993 Nobel Peace Prize

b. novelist; 1991 Nobel Prize for literature

c. Anglican archbishop; 1984 Nobel Peace Prize

d. prime minister, later president

e. singer, Malaika, Pata Pata

f. murdered antiapartheid activist

g. did world's first heart transplant

h. actress

i. last apartheid-era president, freed Nelson Mandela

j. dissident playwright

46

 **Nigeria**

These Nigerians have made their marks in a variety of fields: writing, music, and sports. Identify the field each is known in. Write *W* for writer, *M* for musician, or *A* for athlete beside each name.

___ 1. Augustine ("Jay-Jay") Okocha

___ 2. Seal

___ 3. Henry Akinwande

___ 4. Babatunde Olatunji

___ 5. Buchi Emecheta

___ 6. Mary Onyali

___ 7. Ken Saro-Wiwa

___ 8. King Sunny Ade

___ 9. Fela Kuti

___ 10. Nwankwo Kanu

___ 11. Sade

___ 12. Chinua Achebe

___ 13. Wole Soyinka

___ 14. Ben Okri

___ 15. Hakeem Olajuwon

47

© 2004 Walch Publishing

⊕ Mali: Who Am I?

Use the clues given below to identify the person being described.

In 1312, I became ruler of the Mali empire. Under my rule, Mali became the greatest empire in Africa. Timbuktu became a center of Muslim culture and scholarship. I promoted education and trade in Mali, and brought stability to the empire.

In 1324, as a devout Muslim, I made a *hajj*, or pilgrimage to Mecca. My retinue was large—several thousand people, including slaves and servants. They carried 100 camel-loads of gold, each weighing 300 pounds. As I traveled, I spent lavishly and gave generous gifts. One historian said I gave out so much gold in Egypt that its value fell!

On my return to Mali I brought with me an Arabic library, religious scholars, and a fine architect, Al-Sahili. The mosques and palaces Al-Sahili designed helped transform Timbuktu.

My pilgrimage also had effects outside Mali. Apparently that huge retinue and all the gold made a real impression on people. Before then, most people outside Africa had never heard of Mali. But by 1339, two years after my death, Mali appeared on European maps of the world.

Who am I?

Morna: Music of Cape Verde

The Cape Verde Islands lie in the Atlantic Ocean, about 640 km (400 mi) west of the African mainland. When Portuguese sailors found them in 1460, nobody lived there. The Portuguese started a settlement there. They brought mainland Africans as slaves to work the land. By the time Cape Verde became independent in 1975, its culture was a mix of Portuguese and African. Cape Verdeans speak Krioulo, a local dialect that mixes Portuguese and African languages.

The music of Cape Verde also combines these two cultures. One popular musical style is called *morna*. This music originated among the African slaves on Cape Verde. *Morna* combines a slow rhythm with melancholy lyrics, usually written in Krioulo. Compositions are often in a minor key. A *morna* singer is usually accompanied by guitar, violin, accordion, and clarinet. Another common instrument is the *cavaquinho*, a plucked lute. It sounds like a cross between a guitar and a mandolin. The rhythms, lyrics, and instruments combine to create a sad, soulful sound.

Other musical traditions also combine a mournful sound and sorrowful lyrics. Can you think of one that developed in the United States?

49

Eritrea and Ethiopia

For a long time, Eritrea was an Italian colony. In 1962 it became a province of Ethiopia.

Over the decades that followed, Eritrea consistently fought for independence. Ethiopia fought to keep it as a province.

In 1993, after thirty years of fighting, Eritrea became independent.

Think about the geography of East Africa. What geographic reason might Ethiopia have had for wanting to keep Eritrea? Write one or two clear sentences for your answer.

Daily Warm-Ups: World Cultures

50

◪ Yes, We Have No Bananas

The banana. It's a basic in the fruit bowl, and has been for about 10,000 years. For millions of people, it's a staple food. In sub-Saharan Africa, bananas make up almost half the diet of some 70 million people. It's also an important cash crop. About 90 million tons of bananas are grown every year.

But the edible banana is an endangered species. Some scientists think it will be gone within a decade. All edible bananas are clones. They are grown from cuttings and don't produce seeds. Now the plants are being killed by a fungus. No seeds means scientists can't breed resistant bananas.

Researchers are trying two approaches to save the banana. They are trying to stop the fungus. And they are trying to develop new bananas. Scientists in Honduras peeled and sieved 881,000 pounds of bananas. They found a total of fifteen seeds. The next step is to grow plants from these seeds. If they succeed, the bananas they grow may look—and taste—very different from the fruit we know now.

If they don't succeed, the edible banana may disappear completely. How would that affect people in sub-Saharan Africa? What about the rest of the world? Write two or three sentences for your answer.

51

◉ People of Kenya

Most of Kenya's 28 million people are native Africans. But they come from some 40 different ethnic groups. Each group has its own language and customs. For example, the Kikuyu are the largest group—more than one-fifth of the total population. They farm Kenya's southwestern highlands. The Luo make up about one-sixth of the population. They farm and fish on the shores of Lake Victoria, the source of the Nile. Next in size are the Luhya, Kamba, and Kalenjin. About 70 percent of Kenyans belong to one of these groups. Other groups, such as the Meru, Gusii, Embu, and El Molo are smaller. The El Molo, who live on the shore of Lake Turkana, number only about 500.

52

Kenya's ethnic diversity adds richness and texture to the national culture. However, it can also cause problems. This diversity made it harder for Kenya to overthrow the British colonial government. Why do you think this might be? Write two or three sentences for your answer.

◉ Food in South Africa

Modern South Africa has been shaped by food. The original inhabitants were members of the Khoi, San, Xhosa, and Zulu peoples. In the 1600s, Dutch merchants sailed to Malaysia to buy spices. They stopped in South Africa for fresh food and water. By 1652, a Dutch colony had been founded in South Africa. The Dutch were followed by settlers from Germany, France, and other European countries. They imported slaves from Malaysia and Indonesia. Later, laborers came from India. Then, in the late 1700s, England took the colony from the Dutch. All these groups—African, European, and East Asian— have left their mark on South Africa.

Here are some popular South African dishes. See if you can name the culture that each dish originated in. Choose the correct culture from the box for each dish. (Hint: Think about the language each name comes from.)

a. African	b. European	c. East Asian

___1. boerewors—spicy sausage

___2. konfyt—fruit preserves

___3. isophu—bean and corn soup

___4. samosas—triangular filled, deep-fried pastries

___5. sosaties—kebabs

___6. ting—sour porridge made of sorghum

53

Indian Proverbs

Proverbs are a way to pass on culture. One reason they work so well is that they're usually easy to remember. They use vivid images to get an idea across.

Choose one of the Indian proverbs below. Imagine a scene that illustrates it. Then either draw the scene or write one or two sentences describing it.

Don't bargain for fish that are still in the water.

When an elephant is in trouble even a frog will kick him.

Giving advice to a stupid man is like giving salt to a squirrel.

Where there is sunshine, there is also shade.

One man's beard is on fire, and another man warms his hands on it.

Call on God, but row away from the rocks.

When a camel is at the foot of a mountain then judge of his height.

✿ Indian Holidays and Festivals

Thousands of festivals are held in India each year. Some are confined to one region or one religion. Some are celebrated throughout the country. For example, Baisakhi, the Solar New Year, is an important festival in the north of India. People bathe in holy rivers, give thanks for the harvest, and celebrate with fairs, singing, and dancing. Dussehra is different in every region. This ten-day festival celebrates the triumph of good over evil.

Some other well-known Indian festivals are listed in the box. Below are descriptions of each of these festivals. Match each festival to its description.

| Id-ul-Zuha | Diwali | Holi |

1. Celebrated all over India, this holiday is known as The Festival of Lights. Rows of lights welcome Lakshmi, the goddess of wealth, and celebrate Rama's return._____

2. This north Indian celebration of the end of winter is known as the Festival of Color. People splash each other with colored water._____

3. This Muslim festival marks the sacrifice of Abraham with prayers and feasting._____

55

🌐 Indo-Arabic Numerals

The numerals we use today—1, 2, 3—are often called Arabic numerals. But they weren't developed in Arabia; they come from India. They were brought to Europe by Arab traders. That's how they got the name "Arabic."

Until around 1000 C.E., Europeans used Roman numerals. This system used a different symbol for the numbers 1, 5, 10, and so forth. Roman numerals worked well for counting things. But operations like multiplication and division were hard to do.

Indian mathematicians had a different system. The value of each symbol depended on its place in the number. Each place had a value 10 times the place to its right. With a place-value system, something needs to show when a place is empty. Otherwise the number 42 could mean either $(4 \times 10) + 2$ or $(4 \times 100) + 2$. The place marker developed in India was the zero. Putting a zero in 402 makes the meaning of the number clear: it's $(4 \times 100) + 2$.

Arab traders visiting India saw the value of this system and started using it. Soon it spread to Europe. At first, some Europeans saw the new system as a threat. The city-state of Florence passed a law banning the new number system. But the new numbers made calculations so much easier that they were soon in general use.

56

Imagine that you lived in Florence, Italy, when Arabic numerals were introduced. Write a few sentences either for or against the use of Arabic numerals.

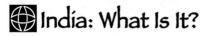

🌐 India: What Is It?

Most countries have landmarks. They can be buildings or natural features. They are sites that people around the world identify with that country.

This is a description of an Indian landmark. Read the description. Then name the landmark being described.

This huge complex of white marble was built in Agra between 1631 and 1648. It is both memorial and tomb for Mumtaz, beloved wife of Mughal emperor Shah Jahan. It is also an architectural gem, with its square base, gently swelling dome, and four minarets, or towers, rising from the corners. Set at the end of a green garden, the building is reflected in the water of a marble tank.

From a distance, the white marble form seems to be pure and simple. A closer look shows that much of its surface is elaborately decorated. Some areas are covered in calligraphy. Other areas use stone inlay to create geometric patterns or floral sprays and arabesques. Still others use intricate stone carving. The jewel of Muslim art in India, this magnificent tomb is universally admired as a masterpiece.

What is it?

57

© 2004 Walch Publishing

 Foods of India

India is a large and varied country. Different regions—Bengal, Punjab, Gujarat—have different customs, clothes, languages, and foods. Some dishes are found in a number of different regions. Some are specific to one place.

The numbered items below describe some popular Indian dishes. Choose the name of each dish from the box. Write it on the line beside the correct description.

chutney nan raita samosa vindaloo

_____1. yogurt-based side dish, often containing cucumbers or other vegetables

_____2. mixture of chopped fruit, vegetables, and spices used as a condiment

_____3. pyramid-shaped, deep-fried pastry filled with potatoes or ground meat

_____4. flat oval bread

_____5. very spicy curry dish

58

English From India

Many English words originally came from languages spoken in India. The Indian words below have all been adopted into English. Match each Indian word on the left with the correct English version on the right.

__ 1. badhna   a. jungle

__ 2. bangla   b. sugar

__ 3. khat   c. bungalow

__ 4. jangal   d. pajamas

__ 5. pajama   e. bandanna

__ 6. sarkara   f. cot

59

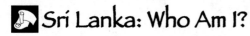

🐾 Sri Lanka: Who Am I?

Use the clues below to identify the person being described.

I was born in 1943 on an island in the Indian Ocean. When I was born, the island was a British colony known as Ceylon. Today it is an independent nation known as Sri Lanka. Like the land where I was born, my heritage is a mixture of Dutch, Tamil, and Sinhalese.

I spent my childhood in Sri Lanka, but moved to England at eleven. At nineteen I started college in Canada; I still live in Canada today.

My first published work was a collection of poetry. Since then I have published novels, poems, and essays. One of my novels, *The English Patient,* was made into a movie in 1996. My latest novel, *Anil's Ghost,* is set in Sri Lanka. It looks at life on the island in the wake of civil war.

Who am I?

Daily Warm-Ups: World Cultures

60

☀ The Ranas of Nepal

Use the words in the box to complete this narrative about politics in Nepal. Choose the correct word for each blank.

hereditary	influence	minister	reform	revolution

In the 1800s, several powerful families had _____ with the king of Nepal. Then, one night in 1847, fighting broke out between different groups. One faction leader survived: Jang Bahadur Rana.

Rana made himself prime _____ and made the position _____. For the next hundred years, Rana's family ran Nepal. The king was a prisoner in his own palace.

In the 1940s, pressure grew for government _____ in Nepal. But the Ranas did nothing. In 1950, King Tribhuvan of Nepal took action. He escaped from his "bodyguards" and fled to India. He demanded that the Ranas return power to him and to the people of Nepal. The Ranas said that he was no longer the king. They named his baby grandson king instead. A _____ broke out in Nepal. By 1951, King Tribuhvan was back in Nepal. For the first time in more than a century, the king had some real say in running the country.

61

Nepal: Who Am I?

Use the clues below to identify the person being described.

I was born and raised as a prince in Nepal, just north of the Indian border. My life was sheltered; I never saw sickness, poverty, or old age.

When I was twenty-nine, I finally saw what life was like for most people. I left my wife and newborn son to find a way to end human suffering.

After years of wandering, I had a moment of insight. I spent the rest of my life sharing that insight with other people. People started to call me "Enlightened One."

More than two thousand years after my death, millions of people all over the world still follow my teachings and look for their own enlightenment.

Who am I?

62

Pakistan: Who Am I?

Use the clues below to identify the person being described.

My father was the leader of Pakistan from 1971 until 1977. Under military dictator Mohammad Zia-ul-Haq, my father was executed. After his death, I was named head of his party, the Pakistan People's Party. I was arrested several times; in all, I spent nearly six years in prison or under detention.

In 1988, I became prime minister of Pakistan—the first woman leader of a Muslim nation in modern history. While I was in office, 1998–1990 and 1993–1996, I tried to end divisions in Pakistani society, including reducing discrimination against women. I began a nationwide program of health and education reform.

I lost my position due to charges of corruption. I maintain that these charges were invented by a political rival.

Who am I?

63

Gandhi and Nonviolent Resistance

"Nonviolent revolution is not a program of seizure of power. It is a program of transformation of relationships, ending in a peaceful transfer of power."
—Mahatma Gandhi

Mohandas Gandhi was one of the most respected leaders of the 1900s. He was given the name "Mahatma." This means "great soul." Gandhi led the movement to gain India's independence from Britain. Gandhi developed ways to protest and resist without fighting. He called his approach *satyagraha*, which means "truth force." People refused to work, or refused to obey laws they considered unjust. They used hunger strikes to bring attention to their cause.

Eventually, Britain gave India its independence. Just a year later, Gandhi was killed by an assassin.

Gandhi's teachings still influence others. During the 1950s and 1960s, two important American civil rights leaders followed Gandhi's example. One used nonviolent resistance and boycotts to obtain rights for African Americans. The other used these methods to improve conditions for migrant farm workers. Can you name these two leaders?

🎭 Performing Arts of Sri Lanka

The people of Sri Lanka have developed many different forms of performing arts. Some of them combine dance, theater, ritual, and masks.

Some of these performance types are given in the box. Write each name on the line next to its description.

kolam	nadagama	sanniya yakuma	sokari

_____ 1. traditional dance ritual to drive out illness

_____ 2. masked folk theater

_____ 3. devotional performance offered to goddess Pattini

_____ 4. folk theater; one play takes a week to perform

65

Think about these performance types. What do you tell you about Sri Lankan culture?

🎵 Performing Arts of India

Indian theater is said to have been invented by Brahma, the god of creation. In all its forms—dance, drama, puppetry—Indian theater today still tells stories from Hindu myths and legends.

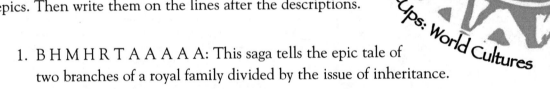

Below are descriptions of two Indian epics. Many plays and other performances are based on stories from these epics. Unscramble the titles of these epics. Then write them on the lines after the descriptions.

1. B H M H R T A A A A A: This saga tells the epic tale of two branches of a royal family divided by the issue of inheritance.

   _____

66

2. M A R Y A A N A: This tells the story of the god-king Rama and his wife Sita, separated by a demon but reunited with the help of the monkey-king Hanuman. _____

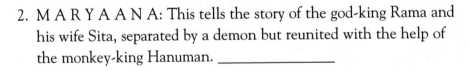

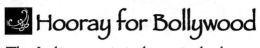

Hooray for Bollywood

The Indian movie industry is the largest in the world. It produces 800–1,000 films per year. (Hollywood produces 250–300 commercial movies every year.) Most of India's movies are made in the city of Mumbai, formerly known as "Bombay." The film industry there is known as "Bollywood."

Bollywood movies come in all genres: romance, drama, action. Bollywood has been described as "James Bond meets *The Sound of Music*." All these movies include traditional Indian music, epic dance numbers, and intricate plot twists.

These lush movies have a broad influence. About 15 million people a day watch Bollywood films. While many Bollywood fans are in India, there are also millions in the rest of the world. Some 10 to 15 million people of Indian background live outside India. For many of them, Indian movies offer a way to connect with their homeland. They show traditional Indian families and values, emphasizing courage, honesty, and respect for elders.

Of course, "Bollywood" as a place doesn't really exist. The word is a combination of two place names. What are those two places?

67

The River Deltas of Bangladesh

Bangladesh lies in the angle of land between the Indian subcontinent and Southeast Asia. It straddles the deltas of two rivers, the Ganges and the Brahmaputra. Most of the land is flat; the highest point in the country is just 1,220 m (4,000 ft) above sea level.

The two river deltas that stretch across Bangladesh are a valuable resource. The rivers deposit rich soil on the land. This soil is useful for agriculture. However, the rivers are also a hazard.

Think about the geography of Bangladesh. How do you think its rivers could be a hazard? List as many things as you can think of.

68

Daily Warm-Ups: World Cultures

🌀 Bhutan and the Age of the Internet

Bhutan is a small kingdom perched high in the Himalayas. Bhutan's kings have tried to preserve their country's culture. To reduce outside influences, contact with outsiders was limited. Until 1961, Bhutan had no diplomatic relations with any other country. Even today, only a few thousand tourists a year are allowed to visit.

Within the country, laws aim to maintain Bhutan's culture. For example, the official dress of Bhutan is the robelike *gho* for men and the apronlike *kira* for women. Any Bhutanese not wearing official dress can be detained.

In 1998, Bhutan's king declared that the nation's guiding principle was Gross National Happiness. To promote that happiness, he opened the country to television and the Internet. People in Bhutan now watch more than forty cable television channels, such as MTV, ESPN, HBO, and CNN.

How do you think cable television and the Internet will affect this remote kingdom? Will they contribute to Bhutan's Gross National Happiness or not? Give your opinion in two or three sentences.

69

© 2004 Walch Publishing

◙ Governments in South Asia

The countries of South Asia are listed below. Choose the correct government type from the box for each one. Then write the letter on the line beside each country.

a. constitutional monarchy	d. parliamentary democracy
b. federal republic	e. republic
c. monarchy	

___ 1. Bangladesh   ___ 5. Nepal

___ 2. Bhutan   ___ 6. Pakistan

___ 3. India   ___ 7. Sri Lanka

___ 4. Maldives

Daily Warm-Ups: World Cultures

70

© 2004 Walch Publishing

 Vietnamese Proverbs

Many cultures use proverbs to teach values and ethics. You may have heard the proverb, "The early bird catches the worm." This is a way of saying that it is better to be early than to be late. Other virtues may also be found in proverbs: honesty, respect for parents, hard work, and so on.

Each Vietnamese proverb below stresses the importance of some virtue. Read the proverbs carefully. Then say what virtue each one suggests.

1. Fold your tongue seven times before you speak.

2. Though he eats alone, he calls the whole village to help launch his boat.

3. When eating fruit, remember who planted the tree; when drinking clear water, remember who dug the well.

4. If you say you will do nine things, then try to deliver ten things; if you say you will do ten and deliver only nine, you subject yourself to derision.

Thai Proverbs

These proverbs are heard in Thailand. Like proverbs everywhere, they give a lot of information about the culture.

Read the proverbs carefully. Look for information they give about geography, climate, arts, and so forth. Then list all the information you find. What can you tell about Thailand from this information?

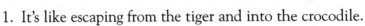

1. It's like escaping from the tiger and into the crocodile.

2. It's like playing the violin for the water buffalo to listen to.

3. It's like taking coconuts to sell in the orchard.

4. Don't worry yourself about the fever before it arrives.

5. Those who can't dance blame it on the flute and the drum.

6. One rotten fish makes the whole catch smell.

72

 Indonesian Customs

Each culture has its own customs and manners. Here are some things that are considered good manners in Indonesia. Choose the category in the box that best describes each example. Write the letter of the category on the line.

| a. conversation | b. greetings | c. public manners | d. table manners |

____ 1. Do not ask how much someone earns.

____ 2. Remove shoes before going into a holy place, such as a mosque.

____ 3. When introduced for the first time, both men and women shake hands and bow the head slightly.

____ 4. Do not use the left hand to shake hands, touch others, point, eat food, or receive an object.

____ 5. Do not use gestures to call someone.

____ 6. Speak softly.

____ 7. When introduced to an older person, a slight bow is polite.

____ 8. Keep both hands on the table while eating.

____ 9. Do not eat or drink before your host asks you to.

✿ Cambodian New Year

All over the world, people welcome the new year. Cambodian New Year is celebrated on April 13 or 14, at the end of the dry season. It is called Chaul Chnam Thmey, "Entering the New Year."

The celebration lasts three days. On the first day people set up altars in their homes. These altars will welcome the New Angel, the guardian of the new year. Families pray for health, happiness, and good crops. Then they visit the temple, wearing new clothes and bringing food for the monks. In the afternoon, they play traditional games. In the evening, the community begins to build a sand mountain. Each person adds a little sand to the pile to ensure health and happiness in the new year. On the second day, children show respect to their elders by giving them gifts. They then play games, dance, and sing at the temple. On the third day, the monks bless the sand mountain. Statues of the Buddha are bathed with perfumed water. Once the statues are cleaned, people sprinkle perfumed water on themselves and each other, spreading joy and good wishes.

74

How is Chaul Chnam Thmey similar to the way you celebrate the new year? How is it different? Write down as many similarities and differences as you can think of.

⊕ Cambodia: What Is It?

Most countries have landmarks. They can be buildings or natural features. They are sites that people around the world identify with that country.

This is a description of a Cambodian landmark. Read the description. Then name the landmark being described.

Built by King Suryavarman in the twelfth century C.E., this temple complex was designed as a stone reflection of the cosmic universe. The great pyramid of stone at its center represents the magic mountain, Mount Meru. The moat and causeways represent the oceans and plains around the mountain. Its soaring towers and miles of courtyards and avenues are decorated with carvings. These carvings tell the stories of Hindu mythology. The largest religious monument in the world, it is also an architectural marvel.

What is it?

75

 Words from Malay

These words came into English from languages spoken in Southeast Asia. Match each word in the box with its meaning in English below.

amok	batik	gecko
bamboo	cockatoo	gong
bantam	compound	sarong

_____ 1. resist-printed fabric

_____ 2. bell that is struck with a padded hammer

_____ 3. large crested parrot

_____ 4. hollow, woody stem used for building and for furniture

_____ 5. enclosure

_____ 6. long strip of cloth used as a loose garment

_____ 7. small, combative person

_____ 8. tropical lizard

_____ 9. out of control

76

1954: Battle of Dien Bien Phu

Vietnam was a French colony before World War II. After the war, France wanted to take control again. But Vietnamese nationalists demanded independence. Nationalists in the Indochinese Communist Party, later known as the Vietminh, declared the formation of the Democratic Republic of Vietnam.

For several years after WWII ended, France and the Vietminh fought for control. The Vietminh used guerrilla tactics, which the French found hard to stop. In 1954, peace talks were scheduled. But France still hoped to defeat the Vietminh. French military commanders chose Dien Bien Phu as the place to lure the Vietminh into battle. Dien Bien Phu was a small village in northwestern Vietnam, near the borders of Laos and China. The French believed their paratroopers, armored vehicles, and bombers would finally destroy the Vietminh.

The French underestimated the determination of the Vietminh. In a battle described as "170 days of confrontation, 57 days of hell," the Vietminh defeated the French.

This battle changed the course of history in Vietnam. Write two or three sentences explaining its importance.

77

⊕ Burma: Who Am I?

Use the clues below to identify the person being described.

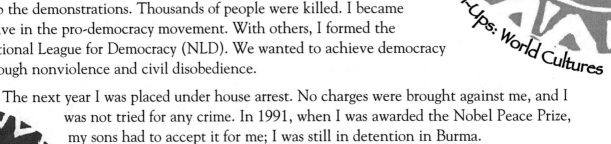

I was born in 1945 in Rangoon, Burma (now known as Myanmar). I went to high school in India, then went to university in England.

In 1988, the military dictator of Burma resigned. Demonstrations followed, calling for democratic rule. The military used violence to stop the demonstrations. Thousands of people were killed. I became active in the pro-democracy movement. With others, I formed the National League for Democracy (NLD). We wanted to achieve democracy through nonviolence and civil disobedience.

The next year I was placed under house arrest. No charges were brought against me, and I was not tried for any crime. In 1991, when I was awarded the Nobel Peace Prize, my sons had to accept it for me; I was still in detention in Burma.

In 1995, after six years of detention, I was released from house arrest. However, my movements within Burma are still restricted. If I try to go anywhere, my car is seized and I am forced to return home. My husband died of cancer in London in 1999. His last request was to visit me; the military junta in Burma refused. We had not seen each other since 1995.

Who am I?

Wayang Kulit: Shadow Puppets

Wayang kulit, or shadow puppetry, is an important art form in Indonesia. Complete the description below by choosing the right word from the box for each blank.

dalang   *gamelan* orchestra   *Mahabharata*   myths   water buffalo

Shadow theater puppets are usually flat shapes made of leather, often from _____ hide. Where the hide is cut away, light can shine through. The puppet theater is a white screen. A light is shone on the screen from behind. When a puppet is placed between the light and the screen, it casts a detailed shadow on the fabric.

The stories of *wayang kulit* usually come from the great Hindu _____ and epics, such as the _____ and the *Ramayana.* The music is played by a _____. The _____, or puppeteer, handles all the puppets and speaks all the voices. In a single play, this may mean handling—and speaking for—up to 100 puppets!

79

 The Mekong River

The Mekong River is the tenth largest in the world. It rises in Tibet and flows 4,186 km (2,600 mi) through Laos, Cambodia, and Vietnam before reaching the South China Sea. In Cambodia, the river flows for about 507 km (315 mi) through the central plain. Every year, the river floods. As much as one-fifth of the land of Cambodia is affected by this annual flooding.

Floods can be disasters. But for Cambodia, this annual flooding is a boon. Why do you think this is? (Hint: Think about Cambodia's main source of food.) Write one or two clear sentences for your answer.

80

Indonesia: Unity in Diversity

The Republic of Indonesia is an archipelago of about 17,000 islands. It is located between the Indian and Pacific Oceans. Only about 6,000 of the islands are inhabited. In fact, about half the population of Indonesia lives on the largest island, Java.

Indonesia's state motto is *Bhinneka tunggal ika*. In English, this means "Unity in diversity." Why do you think this motto was chosen? Write one or two sentences in explanation.

81

© 2004 Walch Publishing

Buildings of Malaysia

Malaysian architecture has always aimed high. In 1996, the Petronas towers of Kuala Lumpur were completed. At 456 m (1,483 ft) each, these towers are the tallest buildings in the world.

Malaysia's traditional houses were also high-rises—after a fashion. They were built on stilts, 3–4.5 m (10–15 ft) above the ground. Different housing styles developed in each part of Malaysia, but they had some things in common. The houses were usually rectangular, with low walls and lots of windows. The high, peaked roof had deep eaves that overhung the walls. Walls and roof were made of wood or bamboo, materials that don't retain heat. Inside, the houses had few walls or interior partitions.

82

This housing style was well suited to the environment of Malaysia. Think about the Malaysian climate. How would traditional Malay houses be suitable for this climate?

 Moped Madness

It's a common sight in Hanoi: A man rides along on a moped, his wife and small son perched behind him, while he holds a pane of glass with one hand. A furniture store delivery driver is delivering a new table—by moped. A family of five goes for an outing on a single moped, the older children hanging on while the baby sits on its mother's lap.

Mopeds are the most common motor vehicle in Vietnam. For a population of about 80 million, there are some 4 million mopeds. There are only about 150,000 private cars. In larger cities, most traffic congestion is caused by mopeds, since there are so few private cars.

Why do you think mopeds are so much more common than cars in Vietnam? Write one or two sentences for your answer.

83

◉ Governments in Southeast Asia

These are the countries of Southeast Asia. Choose the correct government type from the box for each one. Then write the letter on the line beside each country.

a. Communist state	c. military	e. republic
b. sultanate	d. monarchy	

___ 1. Brunei   ___ 6. Malaysia

___ 2. Burma   ___ 7. Philippines

___ 3. Cambodia   ___ 8. Singapore

___ 4. Indonesia   ___ 9. Thailand

___ 5. Laos   ___10. Vietnam

84

Daily Warm-Ups: World Cultures

Proverbs of Palau

The Republic of Palau is a cluster of islands in the North Pacific Ocean. Palauans have adapted to an international economy. But they have also kept many earlier traditions. Villages are still organized around clans, with clan membership coming through the mother. Japanese and American food are popular, but so are traditional Palauan foods, such as coconut and seafood.

Another aspect of Palauan tradition is still strong today. It is suggested by these Palauan proverbs. Read the proverbs and their explanations. What do they tell you about traditional Palauan culture? Write one or two sentences for your answer.

A good leader is like rain that calms the ocean. (A good leader can easily settle arguments and calm people down.)

He's like the chambered nautilus whose shell is very fragile. (He is easily irritated.)

He's like the octopus, which keeps changing color. (He's too easily persuaded.)

You're like the man who uses clouds to mark the locations of his fishtraps. (You depend too much on unreliable people.)

85

✿ Australia: People of the Bleaching

From the 1880s to the 1970s, the Australian government forcibly removed thousands of Aboriginal children from their families. These stolen children are known as "People of the Bleaching" or the "Stolen Generation."

The Australian government has refused to issue a formal apology. Prime minister John Howard has said, "We don't think it's appropriate for the current generation of Australians to apologize for the injustices committed by past generations."

However, many Australians have come together to hold Sorry Days, days to apologize publicly. More than half a million people took part in the first Sorry Day, held in 1998. One Stolen Generation woman, Wendy Hermeston, commented, "This is about the restoration of moral order, about the soul of a country. Saying sorry can help this process because it shows compassion and empathy—not sorry where guilt and blame is proportioned, but where grief is met with comfort."

86

John Howard and Wendy Hermeston offer different opinions about the value of saying "sorry." Which do you agree with most? Write a paragraph explaining your opinion.

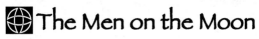 # The Men on the Moon

It was 9:56 P.M. in Houston on July 21, 1969. Neil Armstrong became the first person to set foot on the moon. All over the world, fascinated viewers were glued to their televisions. Few realized that the first images they saw came through Honeysuckle Creek, Australia.

NASA had three 75-m (210-ft) satellite antennae to track the moon landing. The sites were in Madrid, Spain; Parkes, Australia; and Goldstone, California. The schedule called for receiving the images at the sites in California and Australia.

Once the *Eagle* landed on the moon, the astronauts left the capsule earlier than planned. A problem at Goldstone resulted in a poor image. But the angle of the moon meant that Parkes couldn't yet pick up the signal. Honeysuckle Creek, southeast of Parkes, only had a 26-m (85-ft) antenna. But it was locked onto the lunar module's signal. Once the Parkes dish was able to pick up the signal, transmission switched to the larger antenna. But for those first few minutes, the images that flashed around the world came from Honeysuckle Creek.

Why do you think NASA chose sites in Australia, California, and Spain for satellite dishes? Think about how these locations relate to one another. Then write one or two sentences explaining why these three sites were chosen.

🌐 Australia: What Is It?

Most countries have landmarks. They can be buildings or natural features. They are sites that people around the world identify with that country.

This is a description of an Australian landmark. Read the description. Then name the landmark being described.

Rising 348 m (1,050 ft) from the desert, and measuring some 9 km (6 mi) around, this strange formation is the world's largest monolith. Depending on weather and the time of day, the folds of its weathered sandstone change color. It can look anything from blue to glowing red.

This rock formation has two names. One was given to it by Europeans. The other was given by Aboriginal Australians, to whom it is a sacred place.

What is it?

88

"Hello" in the Solomon Islands

The Solomon Islands stretch for 1,920 km (1,200 mi) in the South Pacific Ocean, east of Papua New Guinea. The nation is made up of six large volcanic islands and more than 900 smaller islands. Some are no more than a coral reef.

In area, these islands total less than the state of Maryland. Still, some 120 languages are spoken there. Languages include Rennellese, Maringe, Kwara'ae, 'Are'are, Kwaio, and Pijin English.

Here are ways to say "hello" in several languages spoken in the Solomon Islands. Try saying each greeting. Then write one or two sentences explaining why you think so many languages developed in a country with such a small land area.

Language	Greeting	Pronunciation
Pijin English	monay	(mon nay) (from "good morning")
Rennellese	gaoi	(gah oo ee)
Maringe	keli fara	(kelly far a)

Daily Warm-Ups: World Cultures

89

What's in a Name?

What is the best way to refer to the native peoples of Australia? The English in Australia called them "Aborigines." This means "there from the beginning."

Many Australian Aboriginal people dislike this term. Some prefer the word "Aboriginal," used as an adjective. Others use words in their local languages to describe themselves. This is often the word for "person" in the local language. For example, in southeastern Australia, *Koori*, which means "our people," is used. In south and central Queensland, the word used most is *Murri*. It's *Bama* in north Queensland, *Nunga* in southern South Australia, *Noongar* around Perth, *Wongi* in the Kalgoorlie region, *Yolngu* in Arnhem Land, *Anangu* in central Australia, *Yuin* on the south coast of New South Wales, and *Palawa* in Tasmania.

90

Why do you think many indigenous Australians object to being called "Aborigines"? Write two or three sentences to explain your answer.

# A Capital City for Australia

In 1901, the six independent Australian colonies joined together to form the Commonwealth of Australia. Each colony had its own capital. To prevent rivalry, the Commonwealth agreed to set up a new capital.

The government chose a site for the capital, in the Canberra district. The next challenge was to have the city designed. Australia wanted a capital city that would be a center for government and administration. It should also project an image of the new nation.

They held a competition to design the new city. Competitors were given information about the topography, climate, and geology of the site. They were also asked to include areas for commercial, residential, and industrial use, and to provide for public transportation. In all, 137 entries were received. The winning design was from an American architect, Walter Burley Griffin.

Competitors were given a list of specific buildings and facilities to include. If you were involved in designing a new capital city, what buildings do you think would be required? Name as many buildings and facilities as you can.

⊛ Notable New Zealanders

These New Zealanders are known around the world for their achievements. Match each name with the description of what he or she did.

___ 1. Peter Arnett   ___ 5. Peter Jackson

___ 2. Dame Kiri Te Kanaw   ___ 6. Naomi James

___ 3. Ernest Rutherford   ___ 7. Anna Paquin

___ 4. Sir Edmund Hillary

a. director; *The Lord of the Rings* trilogy

b. Oscar-winning actress

c. war correspondent, journalist

d. first person to split atom

e. opera singer

f. first to climb Mount Everest

g. first woman to sail solo around the world

92

Art of the Australian Desert

Traditionally, the art of the Australian desert was used in ceremonies. Artists drew in the sand or painted on rock walls to pass on traditional knowledge. These paintings could only be seen by people who had reached a certain level of knowledge.

During the 1970s, acrylic paints were introduced. Artists quickly adopted this new medium. They began to create paintings for public viewing, not just for ceremonial use. Their subjects are usually mythical landscapes. Paintings tell the stories of the people who make them. These new paintings still use the symbols and signs of traditional painting, such as dots, concentric circles, and straight or wavy lines. Wavy lines usually symbolize water or rain. Concentric circles usually indicate campsites or water holes. So a pair of concentric circles joined by wavy lines could show two water holes connected by running water.

The symbols of Australian desert art express important information about the environment, such as water, plants, animals, and good places to camp. How would you show the important elements of your life in symbols? Think about the most important things in your life and your environment. Then draw or describe simple symbols to express three or four of these elements.

93

 # Maori Place Names

When English explorers first came to New Zealand, the islands had been inhabited for centuries by the Maori. This Maori heritage can still be seen in many place names in New Zealand.

Here are some Maori words and their meanings in English. Use them to figure out the meanings of the mountain names below. Can you tell what kind of mountains these are?

Maori	English
naki	moving
pehu	exploding
rangi	air
roto	lake
rua	hole
toto	blood-red
tara	peak
wera	burning

New Zealand Mountains

1. Rangitoto _____

2. Rotorua _____

3. Ruapehu _____

4. Taranaki _____

5. Tarawera _____

94

 Australian Cities

Australia's major cities are all near the coasts. Australia's capital, Canberra, is on the east coast. So are Sydney (Australia's largest city) and Brisbane. Melbourne and Adelaide are on the south coast. Hobart is on the island of Tasmania, just off the southern coast of the mainland. Perth is the largest city on the west coast. Darwin is on the north coast.

If you look carefully at these locations, you should see several patterns. Think about these patterns, and what you know about Australia's geography and climate. Why do you think Australia's cities are located where they are? Write two or three sentences for your answer.

95

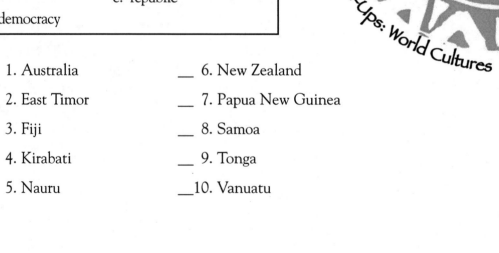Governments in the Pacific Region

These are some of the countries of the Pacific Region. Choose the correct government type from the box for each one. Then write the letter on the line beside each country.

a. constitutional monarchy	d. parliamentary republic
b. federation	e. republic
c. parliamentary democracy	

___ 1. Australia   ___ 6. New Zealand

___ 2. East Timor   ___ 7. Papua New Guinea

___ 3. Fiji   ___ 8. Samoa

___ 4. Kirabati   ___ 9. Tonga

___ 5. Nauru   ___10. Vanuatu

96

☖ Chinese Proverbs

Many cultures use proverbs to teach values and ethics. You may have heard the proverb, "A penny saved is a penny earned." This is a way of saying that being thrifty is a good thing. Other virtues may also be found in proverbs: honesty, respect for parents, hard work, and so on.

Each Chinese proverb below addresses one of the virtues in the box. Read each proverb carefully. Then write the letter of the virtue that best matches the proverb on the line provided.

a. education b. forethought c. gratitude d. hard work e. honesty

__ 1. Talk does not cook rice.

__ 2. Clear conscience never fears midnight knocking.

__ 3. Forget injuries; never forget kindnesses.

__ 4. A sly rabbit will have three openings to its den.

__ 5. The man who waits for roast duck to fly into his mouth must wait a long time.

__ 6. Learning is a treasure that will follow its owner everywhere.

__ 7. Once on a tiger's back, it is hard to alight.

97

⬆ Korean Proverbs

Like those of other cultures, Korean proverbs reflect the customs and values of the people. For example, one proverb says, "After losing a cow, one repairs the barn." This means that it's too late to regret a mistake after we've made it. If we think first, we can avoid misfortunes.

Here are some Korean proverbs. Read them carefully. Then choose one proverb and explain what it means.

1. An empty cart rattles loudly.

2. Even if you know the way, ask one more time.

3. One can build a mountain by collecting specks of dust.

4. The words you speak during the day are heard by birds, and the words you speak at night are heard by mice.

5. When whales fight, shrimps' backs are broken.

6. Even if the sky falls on you, there is a hole from which you can escape.

98

Chinese Myths

Many Chinese myths and legends include a moral—a lesson for readers. Here is one old story. What do you think is the message of this story? Write one or two clear sentences to explain your answer.

Two great mountains once lay south of Jizhou. Yu Gong, the Foolish Old Man of North Mountain, was unhappy that the mountains blocked his way south. He called his whole family together. "I suggest that we level the mountains so as to open a way to the south." His family set to work. They loaded the earth in baskets and carried it to the sea. In a year, they had made one round trip from the mountains to the sea.

Zhi Shou, the Wise Old Man at the River Bend, laughed at Yu Gong. "You are ninety years old, and feeble. How can you remove so much earth and rock?"

Yu Gong replied, "When I die, my son will continue the work, then my grandson. Generation after generation, my descendants will go on digging. The mountains will not grow. Why is it impossible to level them?"

One of the gods repeated this to the Emperor of Heaven. The Emperor was moved by Yu Gong's tenacity. He had the mountains carried away. After this, there were no more mountains between Jizhou and the Han River.

99

 China: Mind Your Manners

Different cultures have different foods and different eating utensils. So it makes sense that they also have different ideas of good table manners.

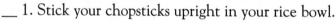

Here are some things you should—and shouldn't—do when eating in China. Put a checkmark (√) beside the items that are considered good manners in China. Put an **X** beside those that are considered bad manners.

Daily Warm-Ups: World Cultures

___ 1. Stick your chopsticks upright in your rice bowl.

___ 2. Use your chopsticks to put food on someone else's plate.

___ 3. Make sure the spout of the teapot is not facing anyone.

___ 4. Order just enough food to go around, with no leftovers.

___ 5. Tap on your bowl with your chopsticks.

___ 6. Serve yourself from the communal dishes on the table.

100

⛰ Body Language in Japan

Body language is used differently in different cultures. Imagine that you're talking to someone. As you talk, the other person nods her head up and down. What is her body language telling you? In the United States, she could be saying that she agrees with what you are saying. But in Japan, this gesture only shows that the person is listening.

Here are some other gestures you might see in Japan. The "meanings" of these gestures are given in the box. Choose the correct meaning for each gesture.

a. anger	c. saying "come here"	e. embarrassment
b. negative response	d. eating	f. indicating oneself

___ 1. touching one's own nose

___ 2. fanning the hand in front of the face as if to fan away flies

___ 3. covering the mouth with one hand

___ 4. pointing the index fingers up from the temples

___ 5. holding an imaginary rice bowl in the left hand while using the right hand to pretend to eat rice with chopsticks

___ 6. waving the hand back and forth with the fingers pointing down

101

Daily Warm-Ups: World Cultures

⛰ Titles in Japan

When you speak to someone else in Japan, you don't just call them by name. You also use a title. In the United States, we might call someone "Ms. Gordon" or "Dr. Wolf." The Japanese system is more complex than this. The title you use for someone depends on how well you know the person. It also depends on whether you are the other person's equal, inferior, or superior.

Here are some Japanese titles and their uses.

San—the most common title; can be used to mean "Mr.," "Mrs.," "Miss," or "Ms."

Sensei—means "born before me"; usually used when speaking to a teacher or supervisor

Kun—used with friends who are the same age or younger

Chan—used when speaking to a child, especially a girl

Choose the correct title to use when speaking to the following people. Write the title on the line after each one.

1. your younger sister _____

2. the principal of your school _____

3. your next-door neighbor _____

4. a classmate _____

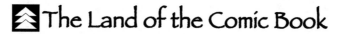

⬙ The Land of the Comic Book

Visitors to Japan are sometimes surprised to see adults reading comic books. But in Japan, comic books—known as *manga*—aren't just for kids. Nearly 40 percent of all printed items in Japan are in comic form.

Much of this is due to one man, Tezuka Ozamu. In 1947 he began to publish *manga* that borrowed ideas from movies. He used close-ups and interesting angles. Instead of showing a movement in a single panel, he used several pages for one movement.

Ozamu didn't restrict himself to simple stories, either. He wrote manga about the mysteries of life. Some of his *manga* ran as long as 1,000 pages. Soon other publishers adopted his approach.

Today there are *manga* for teenagers, college students, and adults. There are *manga* for different genres: science fiction, mysteries, literary classics. There are history *manga,* including *A Manga History of Japan* (*Manga Nihon-no-Rekishi*). This 55-volume *manga* set runs to more than 10,000 pages. It is found in many school libraries.

Why do you think *manga* are so popular? Give as many reasons as you can think of.

103

© 2004 Walch Publishing

❁ Moon Festival

In China, the Moon Festival is held in mid-autumn. At this time, the moon looks bigger than at other times of the year. One story about its origin says that a woman was punished by being banished to the moon. Her husband missed her terribly. One night, when the moon was full, he saw her shape on the surface of the moon. He ran to get cakes to offer his beloved wife. Even now, thousands of years later, people eat round cakes and gaze at the Lady in the Moon.

The Moon Festival is a time of reunion. Whenever they can, families get together. They have moon-gazing parties and eat moon cakes. These are round pastries filled with red bean paste, fruit, or jam. Other round foods are also served, such as grapefruit, pomegranates, and apples. Children make wishes on the Lady in the Moon.

What stories and ideas do you associate with the moon? Think of as many as you can, and write them down.

⊕ Chinese Inventions

Many things we take for granted today were invented hundreds of years ago in China. Some were brought to the West by travelers and merchants. Some were invented later in Europe, without Chinese influence.

Decide whether or not each of these things was first invented in China. Put a checkmark beside each Chinese invention.

__ 1. cast iron

__ 2. compass

__ 3. fireworks

__ 4. gunpowder

__ 5. matches

__ 6. movable type

__ 7. multistage rockets

__ 8. paper

__ 9. paper money

__ 10. photography

__ 11. playing cards

__ 12. refrigerator

__ 13. seismograph

__ 14. sewing machine

__ 15. thermometer

__ 16. umbrella

__ 17. wheelbarrow

__ 18. yo-yo

105

© 2004 Walch Publishing

🌐 China: What Is It?

Most countries have landmarks. They can be buildings or natural features. They are sites that people around the world identify with that country.

This is a description of a Chinese landmark. Read the description. Then name the landmark being described.

This landmark was built to keep northern nomads out of the country. Work on it began around 200 B.C.E. Laborers were forced to work on it; many died. By the time it was finished, centuries after it was begun, it was about 6,400 km (4,000 mi) long. Parts of it were as much as 9 m (30 ft) wide. Some people say that it is the only human-made object visible from space.

What is it?

106

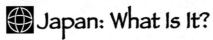

🌐 Japan: What Is It?

Most countries have landmarks. They can be buildings or natural features. They are sites that people around the world identify with that country.

This is a description of a Japanese landmark. Read the description. Then name the landmark being described.

This beautiful volcano is revered as a dwelling place for the gods. At 3,776 m (12,388 ft), it is the highest mountain in Japan. Its last eruption in 1707 created a second peak halfway down its side. Its snow-capped loveliness has made it a frequent subject in Japanese art and literature. Pilgrims have been drawn to its slopes for thousands of years.

Today, it is a popular mountain-climbing destination. During the July–August climbing season, some 400,000 people—often 20,000 a day—head for the summit. Most climb during the night to watch *goraiko*, or sunrise, from the highest point in the Land of the Rising Sun.

What is it?

 Korean Alphabet: Hangul

Until 1446, Koreans used Chinese characters to write their language. The Chinese writing system uses a different character for every word. This makes it hard to learn. Korea's upper class knew how to read and write, but most people did not.

Korea's King Sejong decided to do something about it. He developed a simple alphabet for the Korean language.

Today, King Sejong's alphabet is known as Hangul. Of the twenty-eight letters in the original alphabet, twenty-four are still in use today. Most Koreans are now able to read.

108

English uses the same alphabet as many other languages. But English spelling is confusing. Often, words with very different sounds are spelled the same way—for example, *tough, cough,* and *dough.* Imagine that you are going to design a new alphabet for writing English. How would you go about it? What would your first steps be? Write one or two sentences explaining how you would start.

Gairaigo: Loanwords in Japanese

All languages change over time. As new ideas are introduced, new words develop. Sometimes a language borrows the new words it needs from other languages. The new words are then changed to fit the structure of the "adopting" language.

Over the years, Japanese has borrowed thousands of words from other languages. Borrowed words are called *gairaigo*, "words coming from outside." *Gairaigo* change in several ways to fit into Japanese. All Japanese syllables are made up of a consonant followed by a vowel. So *banana* would be possible as a Japanese word, but *confuse* would not. Vowels would need to be added and the silent "e" replaced—*conufusu*. Some sounds change, too. For example, the "l" sound often changes to "r."

Here are some *gairaigo* based on English words. Match each *gairaigo* in the left column with the correct English word on the right.

___ 1. aachi   a. kitchen

___ 2. adobaisu   b. television

___ 3. terebi   c. yellow

___ 4. kicchin   d. advice

___ 5. kii-boodo   e. keyboard

___ 6. iero   f. arch

109

China's New Words

As new ideas are developed, languages need to develop new words to describe them. In China, there's an extra challenge to developing new words: the words have to be written using Chinese *kanji*, or characters. A simple way to think about *kanji* is that each character stands for a word. If two characters are combined, the meanings of the words are also combined.

To create new words for new ideas and inventions, Chinese has combined existing words to create new meanings. For example, the Chinese word for "telephone" could be read as "electric speech."

Here are the literal translations for some Chinese words. Match each translation with the idea in the box that it stands for.

a. computer	d. microphone	g. movie
b. tissue	e. photocopier	h. VCR
c. elevator	f. tennis	

___ 1. send-talk-instrument

___ 2. duplicate-print-machine

___ 3. electric shadows

___ 4. record-image-machine

___ 5. electric ladder

___ 6. electric brain

___ 7. face-paper-cloth

___ 8. net-ball

© 2004 Walch Publishing

 # Key Dates in Korea's History

Here are some key events in Korea's history. Choose the correct date from the box for each event. Write the date on the line next to the event.

| 2333 B.C.E. | 1392 | 1945 | 1950 |
| 1292 | 1910 | 1948 | 1953 |

_____ 1. Korean War ends

_____ 2. Syngman Rhee becomes first president of South Korea; Kim Il Sung becomes premier of North Korea

_____ 3. China conquers Korea

_____ 4. Korea annexed by Japan

_____ 5. Korea is divided along 38th parallel

_____ 6. Japan invades Korea for the first time

_____ 7. first Korean kingdom is founded

_____ 8. Korean War begins with Communist invasion of South Korea

111

© 2004 Walch Publishing

Korea: Family Reunions

In 1953, the end of the Korean War divided Korea in two. North Korea and South Korea were separated by an area called the Demilitarized Zone (DMZ). Anyone north of the DMZ when the war ended had to stay in the north, and vice versa. This meant that many families were divided. Some family members stayed in North Korea and some in South Korea. About 110,000 South Koreans have relatives in North Korea.

For 50 years, these family members had no contact with one another. Then, in 2000, the first of a series of reunions was set up. About 6,000 people—husbands and wives, mothers and sons, brothers and sisters—have seen one another for the first time in half a century.

Even for these lucky few, the reunions are brief. Relatives get just three days together. Once they return to their own countries, they cannot correspond with one another. No follow-up letters, phone calls, or e-mails are allowed. There are no repeat visits.

Imagine that you are one of these family members, living in either North or South Korea. Write a paragraph describing your reunion with a family member.

⊛ Japan: Matsuo Basho

Matsuo Basho, who lived from about 1644 to 1694, is considered one of Japan's greatest literary figures. The son of a low-ranking samurai, Basho became a samurai himself. When his master died, Basho resigned from service. He spent much of the rest of his life studying Zen Buddhism and writing poetry. Basho is credited with developing the modern haiku form. Haiku are short unrhymed poems, usually no more than seventeen syllables long. They try to capture the sensation of a moment, as in this poem by Basho:

> Old pond.
> A frog leaps into
> the water of sound.

Basho's poetry brought a new spirituality and richness to haiku. He described nature simply, with lightness.

Basho once said, "Learn about pines from the pine, and about bamboo from the bamboo." What do you think he meant by this? Write one or two sentences in explanation.

113

© 2004 Walch Publishing

⊕ China's Revolutionary Leaders

These four men were important figures in China during the twentieth century. Match each name in the box with the correct description.

| Chiang Kai-shek | Mao Zedong | Sun Yat-sen | Zhou Enlai |

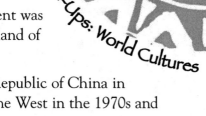

1. Leader of the Kuomintang, or Nationalist Party of China, he gained nominal control of China in 1926. When his government was overthrown by Chinese Communists in 1949, he fled to the island of Taiwan. _____

2. A practical administrator, he became premier of the People's Republic of China in 1949. He helped create China's increased contact with the West in the 1970s and welcomed Richard Nixon to China in 1972. _____

3. The leader of China's Communist Party from 1935 until his death, he is credited with founding the People's Republic of China in 1949. _____

4. Considered the founding father of the Republic of China, he was in exile in the United States when the emperor was overthrown, but returned to become provisional president of the Republic of China. He died before China's unification was complete. _____

114

Arts of Japan

Japanese arts take many forms. Some began as folk entertainments. Others developed out of the Zen Buddhism tradition. Some are considered *shikigaku*, or "ceremonial art." Others are simply entertainment.

Some well-known Japanese arts are listed below. Match each one with the correct description.

___ 1. bunraku   a. flower arranging

___ 2. ikebana   b. serious drama in which men play all roles

___ 3. kabuki   c. woodblock prints

___ 4. origami   d. puppet theater

___ 5. sumi-e   e. paper folding

___ 6. ukiyo-e   f. ink painting

115

Korean Symbols

Many cultures develop symbols that have a clear meaning. For example, in the United States, the eagle is a symbol of pride and freedom. In Korea, visual symbols are used in many ways. They appear on clothes, on pottery, on buildings, and on everything in between.

Here are some of the subjects used in Korean symbols. Can you match each symbol with the idea it represents?

___ 1. bat   a. courage

___ 2. butterfly   b. friendship

___ 3. deer   c. good luck

___ 4. tiger   d. graciousness

___ 5. turtle   e. happiness

___ 6. white heron   f. long life

116

 The Rabbit in the Moon

In the West, people looking at the moon sometimes think they see a man's face. The face is nicknamed The Man in the Moon. In Japan, people see a rabbit. According to legend, a rabbit lives on the moon. He pounds rice into flour and makes rice dumplings. When the moon is full, people on Earth eat rice dumplings, too, sharing in the rabbit's activity.

There is a reason that people in one hemisphere see a man's face and people in another see a rabbit. Can you explain this difference? Write one or two clear sentences for your answer.

117

◉ China: Two Wheels or Four?

The population of China is over one billion. And those billion people own 540 million bicycles. In Beijing, a city of about 13 million people, there are some 11 million bicycles! For decades, the bicycle was the most common form of transportation in the country. Rush hour in the cities, where population density is high, was a solid mass of bicycles.

In recent years, however, car ownership has become more popular. The Chinese government is promoting car ownership. One reason for this is to strengthen the nation's car industry. Another is to give the country a more modern image abroad.

In 1985, there were only about 19,000 privately owned passenger vehicles in China. Today, there are more than 10 million. Now, cars are edging bicycles off the roads—literally. Vehicle accident rates have soared; as many as one-third of all accidents involve cars and bicycles.

118

If the trend of increased car ownership in China continues, what effects might it have? List as many effects, both in China and around the world, as you can.

⬡ Governments in East Asia

These are the countries of East Asia. Choose the correct government type from the box for each one. Then write the letter on the line beside each country.

---

a. Communist state	c. democracy	e. republic
b. constitutional monarchy	d. limited democracy	f. socialist dictatorship

___ 1. China   ___ 5. Mongolia

___ 2. Hong Kong   ___ 6. North Korea

___ 3. Japan   ___ 7. South Korea

___ 4. Macau   ___ 8. Taiwan

119

Russian Proverbs

In proverbs, the message is often hidden. The words may say one thing, but suggest something else. If you don't know the meaning, the proverb can be hard to understand. For example, a proverb in Russia says, "Chickens are counted in autumn." If someone said that to you, what would he or she really mean? Well, chicks are born in spring. Lots of things can go wrong before the birds are ready to sell. They can get sick, or can be stolen. The farmer doesn't plan on money for all the chicks until they've actually lasted till autumn. In the same way, we shouldn't count on success until we've overcome all the obstacles. An English version goes, "Don't count your chickens before they hatch."

120

Here are some more Russian proverbs. Choose one of them. Then write a few sentences explaining what it means.

1. Eggs cannot teach a hen.

2. Do not dig a hole for somebody else; you will fall into it.

3. There will be trouble if the cobbler starts making pies.

4. Stretch your legs according to your clothes.

5. Do not make an elephant out of a fly.

 Folktales from Ukraine

Folktales are enjoyed all over the world. They are used for entertainment. They are also often used to show how people should act. The characters in many stories are animals—but animals that act like humans. These stories often end with a moral, explaining the lesson of the story.

Here is a folktale told in Ukraine. Read the story. Then say what lesson is being taught in the story.

Some wild bees made their home in the hollow of a tree. A bear heard about this bee-tree. He went to the bees and said, "You are tiny and weak, bees, and I am big and strong. You must give me all your honey. If you don't, I'll kill you all and take the honey by force." The bees laughed. "Just try it!" they said. This made the bear angry. He put his head into the hollow tree to eat the honey stored there. Immediately, a cloud of bees flew at him. They stung everywhere they could reach. The bear forgot how strong he was; he turned and ran away as fast as he could. Behind him he heard the bees calling, "Never forget, bear, that even the tiniest creatures can defend themselves."

121

⬛ Writing in Azerbaijan

People in Azerbaijan speak Azeri, a Turkic language. To write Azeri, people used the Arabic alphabet for about 1,000 years. This script wasn't ideal, as it could not really express some Azeri sounds; still, people were used to it. In 1926, a conference on Turkic languages analyzed different scripts. They concluded that, given Turkic sound patterns, the Latin alphabet was the best one for writing these languages. (This is the alphabet used to write English and many other European languages.)

In 1928, under Russian rule, Azerbaijan switched to the Latin alphabet. Then, in 1938, Russian leader Joseph Stalin changed the alphabet again. He was afraid that the Latin alphabet would make it easy for different Turkic-speaking peoples to unite. He insisted that they change to the Cyrillic alphabet used to write Russian.

In 1991, Azerbaijan officially adopted the Latin alphabet—the fourth alphabet switch in less than a century. But the switch from Cyrillic isn't happening all at once. What kinds of challenges do you think are involved in switching the way a language is written? Write down as many problems and challenges as you can think of.

❀ Ukrainian Orthodox Calendar

About 75 percent of people in Ukraine are Christians. Most belong to the Ukrainian Orthodox Church. Ukrainian Orthodox Christians celebrate church holidays on dates different from many other Christian groups. For example, most Christian churches celebrate Christmas on December 25. The Ukrainian Orthodox Church celebrates Christmas on January 7.

This is because the Ukrainian Church still uses the Julian calendar, developed by Julius Caesar in 46 B.C.E. Most other Christian groups use the Gregorian calendar, developed in 1528 to fix problems with the Julian calendar. (The Gregorian calendar is the one used for most secular purposes in Europe and North America.)

In recent years, some Ukrainian Orthodox Christians have asked to change their church's calendar to the Gregorian calendar. They feel that Ukraine must become more European. Other church members want to keep the Julian calendar. They feel that the differences in the calendar are part of their tradition and culture.

In a situation like this, which side would you choose—those in favor of change, or those in favor of tradition? Write a paragraph explaining your opinion.

123

🌐 Lithuanian Amber

Imagine a translucent, honey-colored bead. A mosquito sits inside the bead, apparently ready to bite. But this mosquito has been dead for fifty million years. The bead is made of amber, a drop of fossilized pine resin. The insect was trapped in the sticky resin. Then, in time, the resin hardened it into something like stone.

Lithuania was once known as the Amber Coast because so much amber was found there. From the earliest times, people in Lithuania made amber into jewelry and other ornaments. They have also used it for trade.

124

Today, some scientists are using amber for other purposes. They seek out pieces of amber with "inclusions"—insects trapped in the resin. These insects are often perfectly preserved. What kind of information do you think scientists could get from a fifty-million-year-old bug? Write down as many ideas as you can.

Daily Warm-Ups: World Cultures

🌐 Russia: What Is It?

Most countries have landmarks. They can be buildings or natural features. They are sites that people around the world identify with that country.

This is a description of a Russian landmark. Read the description. Then name the landmark being described.

This unusual cathedral is built of brick. Its central spire is surrounded by eight smaller towers, each topped with an onion-shaped dome. Each dome is unique in terms of shape, pattern, and color.

Although it was built as a church, it is now part of the Moscow museum system. For many visitors it is a visual symbol of Russia.

What is it?

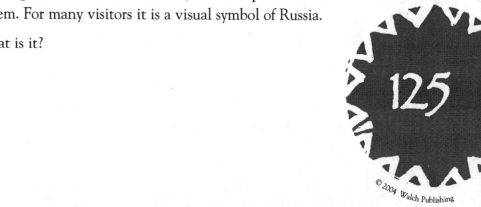

125

© 2004 Walch Publishing

Russia: Who Am I?

Use the clues given below to identify the person being described.

I was born in Russia in 1828, the son of a count. My parents died when I was a child, and I was brought up by relatives. I went to university to study law and oriental languages. But I was disappointed by the level of education and didn't finish my degree. I went home to my estate in the country. A few years later, I joined the army and fought in the Crimean War.

Around the same time, I started my literary career. My most famous novel is *War and Peace*. Set against the background of Napoleon's invasion of Russia, it follows the stories of five families. It includes 580 characters, some real, some fictional.

Even as I started to make a name for myself as an author, I came to see the importance of education. I felt this was the way to change the world. I started a school for peasant children. I kept learning about educational theory and practice, and published magazines and textbooks on the subject.

Eventually, I found I could not be happy living as I did. I left my estate and lived as a wandering ascetic. I died of pneumonia in 1910.

Who am I?

126

Samizdat in the U.S.S.R.

From the 1940s on, the Soviet government tried to control all forms of communication. Certain styles of music were not allowed. Only one newspaper, *Pravda*—the official government newspaper—was available. The only books and journals were those that said what the government wanted people to hear. People's private letters were checked to make sure they didn't say anything the government didn't approve of. Expressing "unsanctioned" ideas led to arrest and years in a labor camp.

Despite the risk, people tried to express their own thoughts and to share them with others. Some wrote books or journals. They had to type each separate copy, since only approved publications could be printed. These books and journals were smuggled from one person to another, from city to city. Anyone caught with these materials could be arrested and sentenced to long prison terms. The Russian word for this kind of underground publishing is *samizdat*. It means "self-publishing."

Imagine that you live in a society where the government controls everything people say. What ways would you find to say what you really think? List as many underground ways to communicate as you can.

127

 Loanwords in Russian

For most of the twentieth century, Russian speakers had very little contact with speakers of other languages. Then, after the fall of the Soviet Union, many barriers came down. A flood of French, German, English, and other foreign words began to enter Russian.

Of course, some sounds common in other languages are not found in Russian. Before they could fit into Russian, these foreign words needed to be changed a bit. Here are some common sound changes:

c → ts
ff → f
t → th
ch → sh
j → zh or dzh
u → yu
y → i

128

The Russian words below have been adopted from English. Use the sound changes above to find the original English words.

_____ 1. dzhas
_____ 2. dzhinsy
_____ 3. menya
_____ 4. metod

_____ 5. ofis
_____ 6. ofitser
_____ 7. parashyut
_____ 8. pizhama

_____ 9. teatr
_____ 10. tsilindr
_____ 11. zhaket
_____ 12. zhyuri

☀ Eras in Russian History

Russian history can be divided into five general periods. Match each period on the left with the correct range of dates on the right.

___ 1. Soviet Era

___ 2. Romanov Dynasty

___ 3. Post-Soviet Years

___ 4. Time of Troubles

___ 5. Rurikid Dynasty

a. about 860–1598

b. about 1605–1613

c. 1613–1917

d. 1917–1991

e. 1991–present

 Boris Yeltsin

From the time he joined the Communist party, Boris Yeltsin was an outspoken reformer. He criticized Soviet leaders for corruption, bureaucracy, and abuses. In 1991, when the Soviet Union broke into independent states, Yeltsin became the leader of the newly independent Russia.

In 1995, Yeltsin said, "We don't appreciate what we have until it's gone. Freedom is like that. It's like air. When you have it, you don't notice it."

What do you think Yeltsin meant by this? Write two or three sentences explaining this statement.

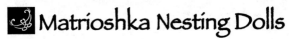

Matrioshka Nesting Dolls

Matrioshka dolls are a well-known example of Russian folk art. They consist of a series of nesting wooden dolls. The largest, usually about 15 cm (6 in) tall, is made in two pieces. Pull these two pieces apart and you find another, slightly different, doll. Inside this doll is another, and another. While a series of five dolls is common, some include as many as forty dolls!

These toys were first made near the end of the nineteenth century. The first matrioshka included eight dolls. The largest doll was a girl carrying a rooster and wearing a *babushka,* or kerchief, on her head. This doll contained a slightly smaller boy doll. The boy contained a smaller girl doll, and so on. The last doll was a baby, wearing a diaper. This is still the classic matrioshka design, but many other designs have been created. Some are based on fairy tales, or traditional folk art. Recently, a popular approach includes dolls based on Russian leaders.

If you were designing a set of matrioshka dolls based on Russian leaders, what leaders would you include? Which leader would be the largest doll, and which the smallest? Name the leaders for a set of at least five dolls, going from largest to smallest. Say why you would include each leader.

131

Lubki: Russian Folk Prints

Under the czars, most Russians could not read. Many people got their information from brightly colored woodcuts called *lubki*. These were popular from the middle of the seventeenth century. *Lubki* combine the style of Russian icons with the ideas of European woodcuts. They were usually painted in bright colors. Captions explaining the story were often part of the design.

At first, *lubki* were used to show events from religious tales. Later, they showed folktales, political propaganda, and moral advice. Sometimes one image would show several scenes of the same event.

Peter the Great used *lubki* to make his reforms popular with the common people. Some *lubki* showed Peter as a folk hero. Some showed scenes of his forced beard-cutting program. Of course, not all printmakers followed Peter's wishes. Some *lubki* made fun of Peter himself!

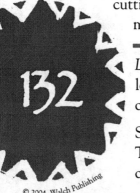

Lubki remained popular until the end of the nineteenth century. As more people learned to read, books and magazines were used to spread the kind of information contained in *lubki*.

Still, the kind of inspiration that created *lubki* is still part of many cultures today. Think about the characteristics of *lubki* described above. Can you think of a communication medium popular today that has many of these characteristics?

Uzbekistan: Geography and History

Uzbekistan lies in central Asia. Much of the country is desert. The western plateau is a region of salt marshes, sinkholes, and caverns. To the east the country rises up into mountains. Only along the river valleys is the land suitable for growing crops.

And yet Uzbekistan has a rich history. Samarqand is more than twenty-five centuries old—one of the oldest cities in the world. Alexander the Great conquered Samarqand. The first paper mill outside China was founded there. Marco Polo came through the city, and it was the home of Tamerlane. The ancient city Bukhara is known for its silk weaving and gold embroidery. Some Muslims consider Bukhara the second holy city of the Muslim world, after Mecca. Tashkent is the capital of Uzbekistan. It has been inhabited since the first century B.C.E. The mathematician Al-Khorezmi, who introduced algebra to Europe, came from Uzbekistan. So did Ibn Sina (sometimes known as "Avicenna"). One of his books, *The Canon of Medicine,* is the most famous single book in the history of medicine.

In part, Uzbekistan's attractions in ancient times were based on its geography. Think about Uzbekistan's location. Why might this have made Uzbekistan so important in the ancient world?

133

Peter the Great and the Baltic Sea

Peter the Great ruled Russia from 1682 to 1725. One of his goals was to make Russia a major European power. He opened Russia up to the West, inviting European engineers and craftsmen to come to Russia. He sent hundreds of Russians to Europe to learn different arts and crafts.

He also kept Russia almost constantly at war. One war was fought against Sweden; it lasted twenty-one years. Through it, Peter achieved a major goal: access to the Baltic Sea.

Why do you think Peter considered it so important to have access to the Baltic Sea? Write one or two sentences for your answer.

134

◉ The Disappearing Aral Sea

Straddling the border between Uzbekistan and Kazakhstan, it was once the world's fourth-largest freshwater lake. Today, the Aral Sea is the most polluted body of water on the planet. In just thirty years, the lake has shrunk to half its former size. It has also become as salty as the ocean.

The Aral Sea is the victim of poor planning. The water from the two main rivers that feed it was diverted to irrigate cotton fields. More water was taken to generate electricity. Projects designed to make up this water loss were never begun. In 1960, the lake covered about 67,000 sq km (26,000 sq mi). Today, the total area of the smaller lakes that remain is about 39,000 sq km (15,000 sq mi).

The shrinking lake has caused many problems in the area. It has affected the ecology, natural resources, local economy, and public health.

Think about the specific ways that the shrinking of the Aral Sea could affect the region. List as many of them as you can.

135

© 2004 Walch Publishing

▲ Czech Proverbs

Proverbs are a way to pass on culture. One reason they work so well is that they're usually easy to remember. They use vivid images to get an idea across.

These proverbs are from the Czech Republic. They compare abstract ideas to actual objects. You can't really have a handful of friends. Work can't have legs. But the comparison makes the idea seem more concrete. It's easy to imagine seeing these ideas as things.

Choose one of the proverbs below. Imagine a scene that illustrates it, showing the ideas as physical objects. Then either draw the scene, or write one or two sentences describing it.

A handful of friends is better than a wagon full of gold.

Wisdom is easy to carry but difficult to gather.

Work won't go away. It has no legs.

No learned person falls from the sky.

Do not protect yourself with a fence, but rather by your friends.

🔺 Food in France

French food is famous around the world. In fact, many English words used in cooking come from French words.

Here are some cooking terms that came from French words. Match each word with the correct definition below.

a. vinaigrette

d. mousse

b. gratin

e. puree

c. mayonnaise

f. sauté

___ 1. smooth paste made by mashing, straining, or chopping food

___ 2. light, creamy dish, made with beaten egg whites or gelatin

___ 3. to cook food quickly in a pan on the stovetop with a small amount of fat

___ 4. dish topped with cheese, then heated under the grill until brown

___ 5. salad dressing made with oil and vinegar

___ 6. creamy, cold sauce made by beating oil and egg yolks; used on salads, sandwiches

137

✿ April Fools and April Fish

In Europe in the sixteenth century, the new year began on April 1. This was when spring and the new agricultural year began. Then, in 1582, Pope Gregory XIII proposed a new calendar. In this system—known as the Gregorian calendar—the new year begins on January 1. The Gregorian calendar became the official calendar in Roman Catholic countries. Eventually, it was adopted in many other countries, too.

France was one of the first countries to adopt the new calendar. Still, the news spread slowly. Some people continued to celebrate the new year on April 1. People who still celebrated the new year in April were called "poissons d'avril," or "April fish." People who celebrated the new year in April became the objects of practical jokes. The idea of April fools spread from France to England, and from there to the United States.

Even today, April 1 in France is called "Poisson d'Avril." A common trick among children is to tape a paper fish to a friend's back, then run away calling "poisson d'avril!" The media report false, but believable, stories.

How do you celebrate April Fool's Day? Is it similar to Poisson d'Avril in France? Write two or three sentences describing the similarities and differences.

138

Olympic Games

Since 1896, the modern Olympic Games have been one of the world's most exciting athletic events. They take their name from Olympia, where the ancient games were held. This was a shrine to the Greek god Zeus. The Olympic Games were part of a religious festival in his honor.

Starting in 776 B.C.E., every four years, athletes from all over the Greek world gathered in Olympia. The Games were open to all freeborn Greek males.

Before the Games, special messengers set off to announce the three-month Olympic truce. This truce meant that travelers heading to the Games would not be attacked. Also, athletes from warring city-states would not attack each other during the Games.

At the end of the Games, the winners were given crowns made of wild olive leaves. Usually, life-size statues were raised to honor them, both at Olympia and in their home city-state.

139

Competing in the Olympic Games was obviously important to the ancient Greeks. Why do you think they valued athletics so much? Write one or two sentences for your answer.

 Science in Europe

These men and women made important contributions to our understanding of ourselves and our world. Match each name on the left with that person's most important contribution on the right.

___ 1. Marie Curie

___ 2. Charles Darwin

___ 3. Sigmund Freud

___ 4. Edward Jenner

___ 5. Joseph Lister

___ 6. Gregor Mendel

a. genetics

b. evolution

c. radioactivity

d. antiseptics and sterilization

e. psychotherapy

f. smallpox vaccine

140

Daily Warm-Ups: World Cultures

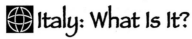

Italy: What Is It?

Most countries have landmarks. They can be buildings or natural features. They are sites that people around the world identify with that country.

This is a description of an Italian landmark. Read the description. Then name the landmark being described.

This tower, built of marble blocks, was designed to be the bell tower of a cathedral. Construction began in 1173 and continued for about two hundred years. Long before it was finished, workers noticed that the tower's weight was making it sink into the soil. Because the soil on one side was softer than on the other, one side sank deeper than the other—about 2 m (6 ft). This gave the cylindrical tower a distinct tilt. And over the last 800 years, the tilt has only gotten worse.

The finished tower is 56 m (182 ft) high, and about 20 m (65 ft) around. Spiral stairs within the cylindrical body give access to the arcaded upper stories and the tower's top. In recent years, engineers have gone into the subsoil around the tower to reduce the tilt, ensuring that the tower will stay standing. But they were careful not to reduce it so much that the tower stands up straight. After all, that gravity-defying tilt gives the tower much of its appeal.

What is it?

141

🐚 European English

The English language has always borrowed from other languages. All the words below have been borrowed from other European languages. The source languages are listed in the box. Match each word with the correct source language.

| a. Dutch | b. French | c. German | d. Italian | e. Spanish |

__ café   __ delicatessen   __ kindergarten

__ canyon   __ easel   __ mosquito

__ cookie   __ garage   __ piano

__ confetti   __ guitar   __ regime

__ cruise   __ hamburger   __ spaghetti

142

 Homer's Heroes

When someone says "Trojan horse," what do you think of? Did you ever wonder where the name came from? Would you have guessed "an ancient Greek poem"?

The poem was Homer's *The Iliad*, which told the story of the Trojan War. Another poem, *The Odyssey*, was about one man's voyage home after the war. The Trojan horse was a trick used to end the war. The Greeks gave the Trojans a huge wooden horse—with armed warriors hidden inside. During the night, they let the rest of the army into the city.

Quite a few English words and phrases come from Homer's poems. Here are descriptions of some of Homer's characters. Think of as many English words or phrases based on these names as you can.

1. Achilles—hero of *The Iliad*; could only be harmed on his heel

2. Mentor—friend who advised Odysseus's son Telemachus

3. Odysseus—Greek hero whose return home took ten years of wandering

4. sirens—nymphs whose singing lured sailors to their deaths

143

☀ The Breakup of Yugoslavia

Before World War I, Yugoslavia didn't exist. Several different groups lived on the Balkan peninsula: Serbs, Croats, Slovenes, Macedonians, Montenegrins, and Bosnian Muslims. Their languages were closely related. But their histories were different. Only two of these groups had independent states. The rest were part of the Austro-Hungarian Empire. A Serb-led movement tried to unify these different groups. This movement was one of the causes of World War I.

Austria-Hungary was defeated in the war. After the war a new nation was created: the Kingdom of the Serbs, Croats, and Slovenes. In 1929 it changed its name to Yugoslavia, "land of the southern Slavs."

144

Right from the start, there were divisions within the new nation. Some ethnic groups resented the Serb leadership and would have preferred an independent country of their own. After World War II, Josip Broz—known as "Tito"—formed a Communist government in Yugoslavia. Tito kept strict control over the country. People with nationalist ideas often wound up in jail.

After Tito's death in 1980, the divisions within Yugoslavia came into the open. In the late 1980s, the country erupted into war. By the time the violence ended, Yugoslavia had split into five separate nations. Name these five countries.

United Kingdom: Who Am I?

Use the clues below to identify the person being described.

I trained as a chemist and lawyer, but I'm best known for my political career. I was elected to the House of Commons in 1959. In 1975 I became leader of the Conservative Party. The next year, a speech about Russia earned me my most famous nickname: The Iron Lady. In 1979 I became Britain's first female prime minister.

As prime minister, I tried to reverse the United Kingdom's economic decline and to reduce the role of government. Many of my actions were unpopular. But my popularity received a surprising boost in 1982. Argentina's military dictatorship sent troops to the Falkland Islands. This is a British colony, which Argentina claimed. I sent a British force to the Falklands and defeated the Argentineans.

Still, I had lost a lot of support. In 1990, faced with divisions in my cabinet, I resigned as prime minister and head of the Conservative Party.

Even today, I bring out strong responses in people. A 2002 television poll placed me as number 16 in a list of "100 Greatest Britons." A 2003 poll, sponsored by another television station, placed me at number three in a list of "100 Worst Britons."

Who am I?

145

Daily Warm-Ups: World Cultures

Who Am I?

Use the clues given below to identify the person geing described.

I was born in 1860 in an area that is now part of the Czech Republic. I started to play the piano at an early age. My first compositions were not received well, so I turned to conducting. By age thirty-one, I was conductor at the Hamburg Opera.

After six years there, I had a chance to be artistic director of the Vienna Opera. However, as a Jew, I knew I wouldn't be hired. I converted to Christianity and got the job. Unfortunately, my music was still not well received. By the early 1900s, I was also being attacked by anti-Semitic newspapers.

In 1907, I was asked to conduct the Metropolitan Opera in New York. The next year, I became the music director of the New York Philharmonic Opera. And in 1910, one of my own compositions was finally a success: my *Symphony No. 8*. By then, I was already ill. I had been diagnosed with heart disease years before. I died in Vienna in 1911.

Although I was best known during my lifetime as a conductor, I am seen today as an important composer. Finally, I have received the recognition I always wanted.

Who am I?

146

 Renaissance Artists

The Renaissance in Europe was a time of great artistic change. Almost every aspect of art was transformed. The work of Renaissance artists still influences art in the West today.

There were two major centers of Renaissance art. One was in Italy. The other was an area of northern Europe. Today, this is part of northern France, Belgium, and the Netherlands.

All the artists listed below were active during the Renaissance. Write **I** beside the name if the artist was part of the Italian Renaissance. Write **N** if the artist was part of the Northern Renaissance.

__ 1. Giovanni Bellini

__ 2. Hieronymus Bosch

__ 3. Sandro Botticelli

__ 4. Pieter Bruegel the Elder

__ 5. Correggio

__ 6. Lucas Cranach

__ 7. Leonardo da Vinci

__ 8. Properzia de Rossi

__ 9. Albrecht Dürer

__10. Artemisia Gentileschi

__11. Michelangelo

__12. Raphael

__13. Peter Paul Rubens

__14. Levina Teerlinc

__15. Titian

__16. Jan van Eyck

147

🌀 Irish Place Names

How do place names develop? They often come from geographical features. A town by a lake might be named "Laketown." One on top of a hill might be named "Hilltop."

Some simplified versions of words in Gaelic, the old language of Ireland, are given in the box. Read the words and their meanings. Then match the town names in the left column with the translations in the right column.

bally—town	carrick—rock	more—big
dub, duff—black	lin—pool	

148

___ 1. Ballyduff   a. big town

___ 2. Ballymore   b. big rock

___ 3. Ballynacarrick   c. black town

___ 4. Carrickduff   d. black pool

___ 5. Carrickmore   e. town of the rock

___ 6. Dublin   f. black rock

 London Fog

What cities do you think of when you hear the word "smog"? Los Angeles? Mexico City? What about London? The word "smog" was invented to describe conditions in London. The city tends to be foggy. Also, by the twelfth century, Londoners were burning soft coal for heat. The coal was cheap to buy. But it didn't burn cleanly. It gave off a lot of smoke, full of tiny bits of black soot. When smoke and fog both filled the air, the bits of soot stuck to the droplets of water in the fog. The result was smog. In London, it was often so thick that people couldn't see across the street. Over the centuries, attempts were made to stop coal-burning. None of them worked.

Then, in 1952, a killer fog hit London. Visibility in the city was almost nil. In one part of the city, people couldn't even see their feet! At least 4,000 people died as a result of the fog.

In response to the smog, the English government passed its first Clean Air Act. Cleaner-burning fuels were introduced. It took time for residents and factories to convert to these fuels. London is still prone to fog today, but it's normal, white fog, not the thick, black fog of the past.

Think about where London is located. How might its location make it liable to fog? Write one or two sentences for your answer.

149

🏵 Wildlife of Eastern Europe

In the years after World War II, Eastern Europe saw little economic development. This caused hardship for many people. But it was a boon for wildlife.

Elsewhere in Europe, farms, roads, railways, and cities cut into open land and forests. Wild animals lost their habitats. In socialist Eastern Europe, this process was slower. Factories were concentrated in industrial areas.

The lack of roads and railways meant that natural landscapes were not broken up. For example, the Carpathian Mountains are home to 481 unique species of plants. Some 8,000 brown bears, 3,000 lynxes, and 4,000 wolves live there. So does nearly half of Europe's population of imperial eagles, a globally threatened species.

Now, however, the region is opening up to the global economy. Eastern European countries are joining the European Union and gaining access to funds for development. Eastern Europe's natural habitat is threatened.

Which aspect of life in Eastern Europe do you think is more important, economic development or maintaining animal habitats? Explain and support your opinion.

150

◈ The Euro

After World War II, some European leaders saw a need for closer ties between the nations of Europe. Six countries formed a union. Called the Common Market, it eased customs duties on coal and iron ore shipped between member nations.

Over the next fifty years, this Common Market expanded. More nations joined. The barriers between nations were gradually dropped.

The Common Market went through several name changes. It is now known as the European Union, or EU. All citizens of EU countries are now citizens of the EU. They have the right to live and work in any member nation. In 2002, most member nations gave up their individual currencies. They now use a common currency, the euro. Even the Greek drachma—which, at about 2,500 years old, was the oldest currency in Europe—gave way to the euro.

What advantages do you think EU nations will find in having a common currency? What would be the disadvantages? Name as many of both as you can.

151

 English Surnames

Some people today go by just one name—Madonna, Cher, Sting. But most of us use at least two names, a given name and a surname. Until the Middle Ages, most Europeans only used one name. They were known by their given names, such as Peter, Richard, and Martha.

This worked well as long as most people lived on farms or in very small villages. But as villages grew into towns, several people might have the same name. It became common to add another name to tell people apart. One approach to adding a name was to name people's jobs, or the place where they lived. Another was to name the person's father, too. Yet another was to use a physical or personality trait.

Here are some common English surnames. Decide how each one probably came about. Then write **J** for job, **F** for father's name, **L** for location, or **T** for trait on the line beside each name.

__ 1. Atwater

__ 2. Baker

__ 3. Brook

__ 4. Carpenter

__ 5. Farmer

__ 6. Ireland

__ 7. Lincoln

__ 8. Little

__ 9. Long

__10. Moody

__11. Richardson

__12. Stern

⬆ Proverbs from Mexico

Sometimes proverbs sound like the punchline of a story. It's easy to imagine someone telling the whole tale, with the proverb at the end.

These proverbs from Mexico sound as if there's more to each story. Choose one proverb. Make sure that you know what the proverb means. Imagine the story that might end with this proverb as the punch line. Then write a paragraph describing the story. Don't forget to write the proverb at the end!

It's not enough to know how to ride—you must also know how to fall.

There is more time than life.

A bird in the hand is worth more than 100 flying.

The dog that doesn't walk doesn't find a bone.

Don't look at the teeth of a horse that was given.

The shrimp that falls asleep gets carried away by the current.

153

🔺 Brazil: *Capoeira*

It's a dance form, a martial art, and a form of protest. It's African and Brazilian. It's *capoeira*.

The word comes from the language of the Tupi-Guarani, one of the original peoples of Brazil. In *capoeira*, dancers "fight" each other to a musical background. They move toward each other, then away, stooping, leaping, never actually touching.

The history of *capoeira* is unclear. The most common story says *capoeira* was developed by African slaves in Brazil. The Portuguese masters did not allow slaves to have weapons or learn how to fight. But the slaves were determined to fight for their freedom. They disguised combat moves as dance steps. Performed to music, these moves looked like graceful dancing. In fact, the dancers were practicing the swings and defense of martial arts.

After slavery ended in Brazil, *capoeira* was outlawed. Then, in the 1930s, a *capoeira* master worked to have *capoeira* recognized as a sport. Today, it is popular in Brazil—and around the world.

154

Capoeira has been described as having elements of the major cultures of Brazil. Write two or three sentences to explain this description.

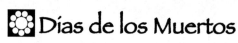

Días de los Muertos

The Mexican celebration of *los Dias de los Muertos*, or Days of the Dead, dates back thousands of years. The Aztecs believed that the dead returned once a year to be fed. Special feasts were prepared for them. When the Spanish came to Mexico, they brought a Christian tradition. They honored the saints on November 1 and honored the dead on November 2. Today's Days of the Dead celebration is a mix of these two traditions.

The Aztec element is seen in skulls and skeletons. Wooden skulls are placed on altars dedicated to the dead. Sugar skulls are eaten. Candles are lit, and all-night vigils are held in cemeteries. People prepare feasts for the dead. The Christian element is seen in the dates—November 1 and 2, All Saints' Day and All Souls' Day—and in the altars that are decorated to honor the dead.

Do you have any traditions that center on this time of the year? What do your traditions have in common with the Days of the Dead? How are they different? Write down as many similarities and differences as you can.

155

🌐 Medicines from the Rain Forest

Malaria is a disease caused by a parasite and spread by mosquitoes. Even today, over 1 million people die of malaria every year. In the 1600s, the death rate was much higher. Then, in the early sixteenth century, European explorers in South America saw native people using the bark of a tree to cure fevers, including malaria. The explorers brought some of the bark back to Europe. The active ingredient in the bark, quinine, is still the best treatment for malaria today.

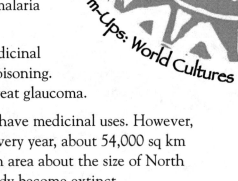

Other plants in the South American rain forests also have medicinal properties. For example, an extract of ipecac is used to treat poisoning. Pilocarpine, which comes from the jaborandi tree, is used to treat glaucoma.

Scientists think that many rain forest plants may have medicinal uses. However, time for the rain forests may be running out. Every year, about 54,000 sq km (21,000 sq mi) of rain forest are cut down—an area about the size of North Carolina. Some plant species may have already become extinct.

156

How do you think people can stop the destruction of the rain forests? Write two or three sentences explaining why the rain forests are being destroyed, and how you think the destruction can be stopped.

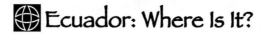

Ecuador: Where Is It?

Use the clues below to identify the place being described.

These islands belong to Ecuador, but they lie out in the Pacific Ocean, about 970 km (600 mi) west of the mainland. They were first settled by Peruvian Indians. In the 1600s and 1700s, pirates used the islands as a hideout. But the islands became famous in 1859 when Charles Darwin published his book, *The Origin of Species*. Darwin was a British naturalist who came to the islands on a scientific expedition. He found some interesting things in the animals of the islands.

All the animals that lived on the islands before people arrived either flew in, swam in, or floated in on drifting wood or plants. Only a few mammals made the trip. But the birds, lizards, and turtles on the islands were fascinating.

One bird species, the finches, particularly interested Darwin. He found several different types of finches on the islands. However, he realized that they had all developed from the same ancestors. Darwin's study of these birds led to his theory of evolution.

Where is it?

157

🌐 Peru: What Is It?

Most countries have landmarks. They can be buildings or natural features. They are sites that people around the world identify with that country.

This is a description of a Peruvian landmark. Read the description. Then name the landmark being described.

This ancient ruined city is perched 2,400 m (8,000 ft) above sea level, high in the Andes Mountains. Built between 1460 and 1470, it once held about 200 buildings, mostly residences. The stones of the buildings were cut with bronze or stone tools and smoothed with sand. The blocks fit together tightly without mortar. Even today, it is not possible to squeeze a knife blade between the blocks. About 1,200 people lived here. They grew maize and potatoes on terraces around the city, using irrigation to reduce erosion and increase the area available for cultivation.

158

There are many mysteries to this mountaintop city. We still don't know why it was built, what it was used for—or what happened to destroy it. But long before the Spanish arrived in Peru, it had already faded. By the time Pizarro arrived in Cuzco in 1532, the city had long been forgotten.

What is it?

 Maya Dialects

Some three million people in Mexico, Guatemala, Honduras, El Salvador, and Belize speak Maya. But they don't all speak the same language; they speak different dialects—more than twenty of them in all. Some of the dialects are so different from one another that speakers of one can't understand speakers of another. Some are spoken by only a handful of people; some—such as Cakchiquel and Kekchi—have hundreds of thousands of speakers.

Linguists believe that, about a thousand years ago, all Maya spoke the same language. Since then, the versions of Maya spoken by different groups have grown further and further apart.

Think about what you know about the areas where Maya dialects are spoken. Why do you think so many different dialects developed out of the single Maya language? Write one or two sentences for your answer.

159

Magical Realism

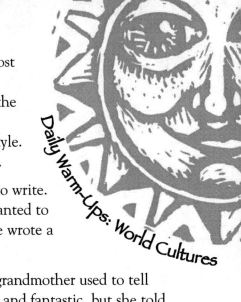

Have you ever tried to tell someone a fantastic story, such as a ghost story? If you told it in a matter-of-fact way, your story might be described as "magical realism." This is how some people describe the work of writers like Jorge Luis Borges of Argentina and Gabriel García Márquez of Colombia. These writers use a clear, realistic style. But the events they describe are sometimes fantastic or dreamlike.

When he was in his late thirties, Márquez had spent years trying to write. He could not seem to find the right approach for the stories he wanted to tell. Then he had a breakthrough. In a yearlong frenzy of work, he wrote a masterpiece, *One Hundred Years of Solitude*.

He later said his tone "was based on the way my grandmother used to tell stories. She told things that sounded supernatural and fantastic, but she told them with complete naturalness. . . . She did not change her expression at all when telling her stories and everyone was surprised. In previous attempts to write, I tried to tell the story without believing in it. I discovered that what I had to do was believe in them myself and write them with the same expression with which my grandmother told them: with a brick face."

Think about the different ways you could tell an unbelievable story. How do you think telling it in a matter-of-fact way would affect the story? Explain your opinion.

 Revolution in Latin America

For several hundred years, European colonial powers ruled Latin America. Then, starting in the late 1700s, a series of revolutions led to independence in most of Latin America.

These are some leaders in Latin America's struggle for independence. Choose one of them. Write one or two sentences about his contributions to Latin-American independence.

Simón Bolívar

Miguel Hidalgo

Bernardo O'Higgins

José de San Martín

François Toussaint-Louverture

161

⊛ Rigoberta Menchú

Rigoberta Menchú comes from Guatemala. Her family were Maya Indians. There are many different branches of Maya, each with its own dialect, dress, and traditions.

The Maya have often been discriminated against. In Guatemala during the 1970s, some Maya formed groups to protest this treatment. These groups were often put down with violence. Rigoberta Menchú's brother, father, and mother were all killed. After this, she began working for rights for indigenous people.

In 1981 she had to go into hiding, then escape to Mexico. In 1983 she told her life story to Elisabeth Burgos Debray. It was published as a book: *I, Rigoberta Menchú*. While in exile from Guatemala, Menchú continued to work for human rights.

In 1992, Rigoberta Menchú became the youngest person ever to receive the Nobel Peace Prize. Commenting on the need for respect for indigenous peoples around the world, Menchú has said, "We are not myths of the past, ruins in the jungle

What do you think Menchú meant by this? Write one or two sentences explaining your answer.

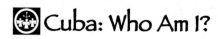

Cuba: Who Am I?

Use the clues given below to identify the person being described.

I was born in 1926 on my family's sugar plantation in Cuba. As a boy, I worked in the sugarcane fields. I went to the University of Havana and became a lawyer. Although I married into a wealthy family, I worked to help the poor of Cuba.

By the time I was in my twenties, I had become an opponent of Cuba's dictator, Fulgencio Batista. I was jailed for an attack on a military barracks. In 1956 I started a guerrilla war against Batista. Finally, in January 1959, Batista fled. In February 1959, I became premier of Cuba.

Soon after, relations between Cuba and the United States soured. I felt that foreign owners did not pay enough for their plantations in Cuba. I began to seize foreign-owned property, putting it in the name of Cuba's government. I also became friendly with the Soviet Union. Eventually, the United States ended diplomatic relations with my government.

Since the Soviet Union collapsed in 1991, Cuba has become isolated. Cuban exiles in Miami predict that I will soon fall from power. But my people remain independent and proud. And they continue to rally behind me as their leader.

Who am I?

163

Murals of Mexico

Mexico has a long tradition of mural painting, or paintings on walls. The Maya, whose civilization reached its peak between 300 and 900 C.E., painted murals on the stone walls of their temples. These murals showed both scenes from real life and stories from Maya myths.

In the early twentieth century, Diego Rivera revived this mural tradition. Unlike other Mexican painters of that time, Rivera rejected the European painting style. He created a Mexican style of painting that reflected his people and culture. He used murals to tell the history of the Mexican people.

Choose an event in Mexican history that you think would be a good subject for a mural. Draw or write a description of the mural.

164

 Geography of Latin America

The geography of Latin America affects life there in both good and bad ways. For example, the three major rivers of South America are the Orinoco, the Amazon, and the Rio de la Plata. These rivers have provided a means of transportation, water for irrigation, and fertile soil for agriculture. However, they also tend to flood. These floods can be very destructive.

Name at least two other important geographic features of Latin America. For each one, describe both its good and bad effects on people's lives.

165

◼ The Yanomamo

The Yanomamo live in the Amazon rain forest of South America. Until the 1980s, they had very little contact with the rest of the world. In 1988, a gold rush brought people to the area. The Yanomamo have suffered from the contact, and their way of life is threatened. These are the words of one of their leaders.

> Everyone likes to give as well as to receive. No one wishes only to receive all the time. We have taken much from your culture. . . . I wish you had taken something from our culture . . . for there were some good and beautiful things in it. (quoted in Breuilly, O'Brien, and Palmer, *Religions of the World*)

What do you think the speaker meant by this quotation? Write one or two sentences to explain it.

166

Ben Franklin's Words of Wisdom

Benjamin Franklin was one of the leaders of the American Revolution. He was also a writer and publisher. He used his printing press to share wise sayings that he hoped would help his readers. Some of these sayings he wrote himself. Some he adapted from other sources.

Here are some of the sayings Franklin published. Read them carefully. Then say what virtues you think Franklin admired.

A lie stands on one leg, the truth on two.

One today is worth two tomorrows.

A quarrelsome man has no good neighbors.

Three may keep a secret, if two of them are dead.

Up, sluggard, and waste not life; in the grave will be sleeping enough.

Early to bed and early to rise makes a man healthy, wealthy, and wise.

An investment in knowledge always pays the best interest.

Never leave that till tomorrow which you can do today.

He that goes a borrowing goes a sorrowing.

167

✺ Let's Celebrate

All around the world, people celebrate holidays. In the United States, most national holidays celebrate an important event or person in the country's history. These include July 4, Thanksgiving, and Memorial Day.

But the United States also has many regional holidays and celebrations. For example, New Orleans celebrates Mardi Gras. New York, San Francisco, and other cities with large Chinese-American populations celebrate the Chinese New Year. Other celebrations are less well known, such as the Paul Bunyan Days in St. Maries, Idaho, or the Tulip Festival in Holland, Michigan. Still, each of these festivals celebrates something distinctive about a region's culture and history.

168

What festivals are unique to your area? What aspect of your region's culture do they celebrate? Draw a picture or write a description of a celebration from your region or another place you have lived. Include an explanation of what aspect of culture is being celebrated.

Gold Rush Pants

The California Gold Rush drew many people who dreamed of making a fortune. One of them was a young German immigrant, Loeb (or Levi) Strauss. He didn't go to California to work in the mines, though; he set up a store selling fabric and other dry goods.

A tailor named Jacob Davis used fabric from this store to make pants for miners. This tough fabric was named for the city in France where it was first made. One problem miners had with their pants was that they often put nuggets in their pockets. The weight ripped the seams. Davis solved this problem. He used metal rivets as well as seams to attach the pockets.

Davis and Strauss went into business together, selling tough pants with riveted pockets; they called them "waist overalls." Today, these pants have another name. It probably comes from the cotton pants worn by Italian sailors.

These pants combine elements from several countries, but the result is American through and through. Match the people and places named below with the words that they gave rise to.

____ 1. Genoa, Italy   a. Levi's

____ 2. Nimes, France   b. jeans

____ 3. Loeb (Levi) Strauss   c. denim

169

⊕ United States: What Is It?

Most countries have landmarks. They can be buildings or natural features. They are sites that people around the world identify with that country.

This is a description of a landmark in the United States. Read the description. Then name the landmark being described.

It started as a riverbed—a long, long time ago. For millions of years, as the Colorado River flowed from the mountains to the sea, it wore away the stone it flowed over. Near the surface, the rock was limestone, formed about 250 million years ago. The river ate its way through that layer and the next, through almost a mile of solid rock.

Today, the Colorado River runs through a gorge that is about 1.6 km (1 mi) deep and an average of 16 km (10 mi) wide. Its vastness, its rugged contours, and the colors of the rock layers, which show the history of the earth, leave visitors spellbound.

What is it?

⊕ Canada: Where Is It?

This site at the tip of a Canadian island lay forgotten for centuries. In 1960, a Norwegian team came to the island. They were looking for traces of Viking settlements. At this site, they found them.

The stone and turf buildings built here were similar in style to buildings in Iceland and Greenland. Artifacts found on the site include a bronze pin like those used by Norsemen.

Archaeologists and anthropologists studied the site. The evidence suggests that this is the site of a Norse settlement from around 995 C.E. It was founded by Thorfinn Karlsefni and Thorvald Eriksson. The first child born to Europeans on the North American continent was born here—almost 500 years before Columbus reached the Caribbean.

Where is it?

171

⬛ Combination Words

English includes words that were created by running two words together, such as "cheeseburger" (a hamburger with cheese) or "smog" (a mixture of smoke and fog).

Here are definitions of some combination words. Try to identify the words from their definitions. Then write the words that were combined to create them.

1. living being whose powers are enhanced by computer implants _____

2. serialized television comedy program _____

3. meal eaten late in the morning _____

4. very, very rough estimate _____

5. roadside hotel _____

6. inflation in an economy with no growth in employment or demand for goods _____

172

Daily Warm-Ups: World Cultures

☀ Events in Canadian History

Here are some important events in Canada's history—in no particular order. Decide what order they took place in. Then number them 1–12, in chronological order.

___ a. John Cabot claims Atlantic Coast for England

___ b. French defeated by British, ending French rule in Canada

___ c. Right to vote in federal elections for Canadian women over age 21

___ d. The boundary between British North America and the United States is set at 49°N.

___ e. Free Trade Agreement between Canada, United States goes into effect

___ f. Cartier lands at Gaspé, claims territory for France

___ g. The St. Lawrence Seaway opens, allowing oceangoing vessels to sail from Lake Superior to Montréal

___ h. Samuel de Champlain sets up a fur trading post at Québec

___ i. Hudson's Bay Company founded, given monopoly of trade

___ j. Cornwallis founds Halifax, creates British foothold in Nova Scotia

___ k. English expel Acadians who refused an oath of allegiance

___ l. Klondike Gold Rush

173

© 2004 Walch Publishing

⊛Revolutionary Leaders

By the late 1700s, many people in the American colonies were unhappy with British rule. A handful of individuals had the vision and the courage to do something about it.

Unscramble the groups of letters below to find the names of some key figures in the American Revolution.

1. N O J H   A M D S A _____

2. U S L A M E   S M D A A _____

3. J A M I N N B E   L I N K F A R N _____

4. N O H J   C H O C K A N _____

5. C P K A R T I   R Y E H N _____

6. M S A O T H   E E F F J N O R S _____

7. A E J M S   I O S T _____

8. S M A T H O   N E P A I _____

9. A L P U   E E E R R V _____

10. R G G E E O   T O N S H I N W A G _____

174

Famous Canadians

The Canadians listed below are known around the world for their work. Decide which field each person is known for. Then write **A** for acting, **L** for literature, **M** for music, or **S** for sports by each name.

___ 1. Margaret Atwood

___ 2. Jim Carrey

___ 3. Robertson Davies

___ 4. Michael J. Fox

___ 5. Wayne Gretzky

___ 6. W. P. Kinsella

___ 7. Diana Krall

___ 8. Stephen Leacock

___ 9. Mario Lemieux

___10. Sarah McLachlan

___11. Alanis Morissette

___12. Maurice "Rocket" Richard

___13. Bobby Orr

___14. Keanu Reeves

___15. Mike Myers

___16. Shania Twain

175

American Music: Jazz

Jazz today is popular all over the world. But its roots are in the United States. In fact, jazz is the first American music to affect music in the rest of the world.

Like the country it comes from, jazz mixes many cultures. Its roots are in the music of Africans brought here as slaves. In the United States, African-American music developed into spirituals, work songs, and the blues. In the late 1800s, four million slaves became American citizens. Their music mixed with other musical traditions, including French, Spanish, and Irish. A rich new musical sound developed: the sound of jazz.

Here are some of the greatest names in twentieth-century jazz. Choose the instrument from the box that is most associated with each name.

cornet	piano	tenor sax	trumpet	voice

1. Louis Armstrong _____

2. Bix Beiderbecke _____

3. John Coltrane _____

4. Miles Davis _____

5. Duke Ellington _____

6. Ella Fitzgerald _____

7. Dizzy Gillespie _____

8. Billie Holiday _____

176

 Conservation President

Theodore Roosevelt was president of the United States from 1901 to 1909. Roosevelt believed that U.S. natural resources should be preserved. He set aside public land to be used as national forests and created the National Wildlife Refuge program. He also created many national parks and monuments. In talking about the Grand Canyon, Roosevelt said:

> Keep it for your children and your children's children, and for all who come after you, as one of the great sights which every American, if he can travel at all, must see.

In all, Roosevelt named five national parks, eight national monuments, one hundred fifty national forests, four national game preserves, and fifty-one national bird sanctuaries. Many places that are national parks and monuments today date back to Roosevelt. Name as many national parks and monuments as you can.

177

◆ Water in the Western United States

In the United States east of the Rocky Mountains, average rainfall is more than 20 inches a year. West of the Rockies, it is less than 20 inches a year. This means that states west of the Rockies depend on rivers for water.

In the eastern states, water rights come with the land. If you own land along a river, you have the right to use the water. In the west, a different approach to water rights developed. It is called the prior appropriation system. This is sometimes described as "first in time, first in right." Basically, the first person to arrive and use the water for a "beneficial use" had the right to keep using that amount of water. The second person to arrive could also get the right to use water. But the first person's rights had first claim.

In a year when the river is low, the first person would get water. The second person might not.

178

What advantages can you see to this system of water rights? What disadvantages can you see? Do you think this system is fair, or unfair? Write three or four sentences explaining your opinion.

✸ Moving to the Suburbs

During the twentieth century, population distribution in the United States changed a great deal. At the start of the century, most people lived in rural areas. By about 1920 half the population lived in urban areas and half lived in rural areas. People either lived and worked in the city, or lived in the country and worked on farms.

During the 1920s and 1930s, suburbs began to grow. In 1950, less than a quarter of people in the United States lived in suburban areas; almost one-third lived in rural areas. By 1990, one half of U.S. residents lived in the suburbs; about one-fifth lived in rural areas.

Of course, many factors led to this change, but one factor had the most influence. What was it? Write one or two sentences to explain your answer.

179

◉ Multilingual Health Care

From the time the first Europeans set foot here, the United States has always been a land of immigrants. Some come here to escape violence and unrest in their birth countries. Some come to pursue an education. Some come to join family members, or to accept a job. Some come for a short time to get medical attention.

One of the first challenges many new residents face is learning the language. Not being able to communicate makes everyday tasks a huge challenge. It can also make dealing with an emergency even harder.

Hospitals in large cities have patients who speak dozens of languages. When health care providers and patients do not speak the same language, the quality of care can suffer. To address this, some hospitals have prepared booklets with useful phrases in English and another language. Phrases include ways to express discomfort and make requests. One hospital may have booklets in more than a dozen languages.

180

Imagine that you are helping prepare a booklet for use with non-English-speaking patients. What kinds of words and phrases would you include? List as many as you can.

Answer Key

181

1. Answers will vary. You may wish to have students brainstorm to list proverbs. Here are a few to get them started. "A bird in the hand is worth two in the bush." "Birds of a feather flock together." "Cut your coat according to your cloth." "Don't change horses in midstream." "Don't count your chickens before they're hatched." "Don't put the cart before the horse." "Good fences make good neighbors." "His bark is worse than his bite." "It's a long lane that has no turning." "The squeaky wheel gets the grease." "Make hay while the sun shines." "Strike while the iron is hot." "You can lead (take) a horse to water, but you can't make it drink." "You can't make a silk purse out of a sow's ear."

2. The problem of the quarter day is solved by adding a day every four years. Most years are 365 days long; every four years, with some exceptions, the four quarters are added together to give one extra day, for a 366-day year. These years are known as "leap years."

3. Answers will vary. Specific new-year celebrations from other parts of the world are covered in other sections of this book.

4. Answers will vary. You may want to share some more detailed availability figures with students. Vehicles per 1,000 inhabitants: United States: 783; Latin America: 88.3; Africa: 22.4; China: 7.9; India: 6.7. Water: 1.1 billion people do not have access to safe water; 2.4 billion do not have access to adequate sanitation; Electricity: 1.64 billion people do not have access to electricity.

5. Student lists will vary.

6. Answers will vary.

7. Answers will vary.

8. Answers will vary.

9. 1. T; 2. T; 3. T; 4. D; 5. D; 6. D; 7. D; 8. T; 9. D; 10. D; 11. D; 12. T

10. Answers will vary.

11. Answers will vary. Sample answer: Being flexible; keeping an open mind and not thinking something is bad just because it's different; having a sense of humor so you can laugh off embarrassing or annoying incidents; coping well with failure, because you're bound to fail at some things in a

Answer Key

different culture; being curious about new people, places, and ideas; being willing to communicate and ask questions; having tolerance for differences; having tolerance for ambiguity; having patience.

12. 1. c; 2. d; 3. b; 4. e; 5. a

13. 1. c; 2. a; 3. d; 4. b

14. One is a lunar calendar, the other is a solar one. The lunar calendar year is 354.36 days long, while the solar year is 365.24 days long. This means that the Islamic year is about 11 days shorter than the Gregorian year—even more in leap years, when the Gregorian calendar adds a day. The Islamic calendar is slowly "gaining" on the Gregorian calendar. So although year 1 A.H. is equivalent to year 622 C.E., eventually, the two calendars will show the same year—in 20874.

15. Answers will vary.

16. Islam: Jerusalem is associated with several of the early prophets; when Muhammad went to Heaven to see God, he rose up from Jerusalem.
Christianity: Jerusalem is the city where Christ was crucified and rose from the dead. Judaism: the

city of King David; Holy Zion, where the promised Messiah will come.

17. The circle is divided into 360 degrees.

18. Hagia Sophia, Istanbul

19. The Great Sphinx at Giza

20. Answers will vary.

21. scarlet; mohair; sofa; apricots; oranges; algebra; magazine; zero

22. Answers will vary. Sample answer: Because they are funny, so people remember them and tell them to other people, spreading the stories. The stories have different levels of meaning. This story looks at things from a different angle. Looking at things differently can help people change rigid thinking patterns, which the Sufis aimed to do.

23. 1. bazaar; 2. spinach; 3. check; 4. magic; 5. khaki

24. Answers will vary.

25. Answers will vary. Sample answer: A text is carved into the stone in three different scripts: hieroglyphics, everyday Egyptian script, and Greek. It was the key to being able to translate hieroglyphics, which has unlocked the history of

Egypt.

26. Answers will vary. Sample answer: He meant that signing the peace agreement was harder than fighting in a war because soldiers are respected for their courage, but people in Israel probably wouldn't approve of a peace treaty, so Begin would get less respect for this than he would for war. Still, he felt that, in the long term, peace was better than war.

27. 1. Palestine Liberation Organization; 2. Syria; 3. Israel; 4. Israel; 5. Jordan; 6. Israel; 7. Egypt; 8. Egypt; 9. Israel; 10. Egypt

28. Answers will vary. Sample answer: Islam considers that creating living things that move, such as humans and animals, is the realm of God. Artists are discouraged from creating such figures in their art.

29. Student calligraphy will vary.

30. 1. tagine; 2. couscous; 3. bisteeya; 4. harissa

31. Answers will vary. Sample answer: Similarities: Both areas were centered on rivers that enabled early farmers to grow crops in arid climates. Both included level land that was suitable for the

development of irrigation. Differences: Egypt was protected from invaders by the desert that lay beyond the Nile Valley, but the desert also kept Egypt from expanding beyond its borders. The floods of the Nile River were regular and predictable, but those of the Tigris and Euphrates were irregular.

32. Answers will vary.

33. 1. g; 2. c; 3. d; 4. f; 5. g; 6. a; 7. c; 8. c; 9. d; 10. c; 11. c; 12. c; 13. e; 14. a; 15. b; 16. d

34. Answers will vary.

35. 1. b; 2. b; 3. c; 4. d; 5. b; 6. a

36. 1. f; 2. d; 3. e; 4. c; 5. b; 6. a

37. Answers will vary.

38. Answers to the first question will vary, depending on the year and time of year. Ethiopia will mark the year 2000 in Gregorian year 2007.

39. Answers will vary. Sample answer: The Leakeys' find changed people's thinking about human origins. Previously, scientists saw human evolution as a single, straight line. This fossil find helped develop the idea that the evolutionary process is much more complex than that. Also, this was the

first significant find made in the Rift Valley, which
has since been a source for many other discoveries.

40. rock-hewn churches of Lalibela

41. Answers will vary. Sample answer: Many different
languages are spoken because different ethnic
groups were included within the borders when the
English territory of Sierra Leone was formed in the
nineteenth century.

42. Answers will vary. Sample answer: Many enslaved
Africans came from West Africa. They brought
their rich oral tradition with them to the
Americas.

43. 1. aipot; 2. fren-fren; 3. dorti-dorti; 4. adonkia;
5. bifor-bifor; 6. melesin; 7. abeg; 8. sawa; 9. tineja;
10. barawo

44. a. 8; b. 2; c. 5; d. 10; e. 3; f. 4; g. 9; h. 7; i. 1; j. 11;
k. 6

45. Answers will vary.

46. 1. g; 2. f; 3. d; 4. i; 5. j; 6. b; 7. e; 8. a; 9. h; 10. c

47. 1. A; 2. M; 3. A; 4. M; 5. W; 6. A; 7. W; 8. M;
9. M; 10. A; 11. M; 12. W; 13. W; 14. W; 15. A

48. Mansa Musa

49. the blues

50. Eritrea lies between Ethiopia and the Gulf of
Aden. Losing Eritrea meant that Ethiopia lost
access to ports on the Red Sea, a major blow to
the landlocked nation's means of transport.

51. Answers will vary. Sample answer: Much of
Africa, Asia, and Central America depends on the
banana for up to half their daily calories. If the
crop falls victim to the fungus, alternative sources
of food will need to be found for millions of
people. Until such sources are found, the loss
could be similar to that when the Irish potato crop
failed in the mid-1800s, with widespread famine.
Also, the financial loss to these regions from the
failure of the crop would be another blow to areas
that are already struggling economically.

52. Answers will vary. Sample answer: It made it
harder for Kenyans from different ethnic groups to
unite under one leader and overthrow their
government. The different languages of the groups
made communication difficult, and their different
geographic locations and occupations meant that

they had very different goals and aims.
53. 1. b; 2. b; 3. a; 4. c; 5. c; 6. a
54. Answers will vary.
55. 1. Diwali; 2. Holi; 3. Id-ul-Zuha
56. Answers will vary.
57. Taj Mahal
58. 1. raita; 2. chutney; 3. samosa; 4. nan; 5. vindaloo
59. 1. e; 2. c; 3. f; 4. a; 5. d; 6. b
60. Michael Ondaatje
61. 1. influence; 2. minister; 3. hereditary; 4. reform; 5. revolution
62. Siddhartha Gautama, known as Buddha, "the Enlightened One"
63. Benazir Bhutto
64. Martin Luther King Jr. and Cesar Chavez
65. Answers will vary. 1. sanniya yakuma; 2. kolam; 3. sokari; 4. nadagama
66. 1. Mahabharata; 2. Ramayana
67. Hollywood and Bombay (now Mumbai)
68. Answers will vary. Sample answer: Most of the country is very low-lying and lies in the path of the monsoons. The combination of flat land, rivers, and heavy rain would lead to heavy flooding, resulting in loss of life and damage to crops and property. Waterborne diseases would be common.
69. Answers will vary. Initial reports from Bhutan suggest that the advent of cable television is adversely affecting many aspects of Bhutanese culture, including an increase in crime and decrease in educational achievement.
70. 1. d; 2. c; 3. b; 4. e; 5. a; 6. b; 7. e
71. Answers will vary. Sample answers: 1. politeness; 2. sharing; 3. gratitude; 4. keeping promises
72. Answers will vary. Sample answer: The proverbs tell us about animals found in Thailand, including the tiger, crocodile, and water buffalo. The tigers and crocodiles indicate jungles and rivers. The proverbs tell us that fishing is part of the Thai economy, indicating that the country is coastal or has many lakes. The coconuts indicate that the climate is subtropical. Proverb 4 suggests that fevers are common in Thailand; perhaps mosquitoes carry malaria or other insect-borne

diseases. The reference to water buffaloes in proverb 2 suggests rice cultivation, as water buffaloes are often used there. Proverbs 2 and 5 tell us that music and dance are part of the culture; specific instruments include the violin, flute, and drum. Overall, the proverbs suggest a subtropical country where fishing and rice cultivation are important, and music and culture are valued.

73. 1. a; 2. c; 3. b; 4. c; 5. c; 6. a; 7. b; 8. d; 9. d
74. Answers will vary.
75. Angkor Wat
76. 1. batik; 2. gong; 3. cockatoo; 4. bamboo; 5. compound; 6. sarong; 7. bantam; 8. gecko; 9. amok
77. Answers will vary. Sample answer: The initiative in Vietnam shifted from the colonial powers to the Vietminh and led to the Geneva Conference of 1954, which created the nations of South and North Vietnam. Fearing that the Communist government of North Vietnam might spread to other countries in Southeast Asia, the U.S.

government began to try to influence the government of South Vietnam. This led eventually to U.S. involvement in the Vietnam War.

78. Aung San Suu Kyi
79. 1. waterbuffalo; 2. myths; 3. *Mahabharata*; 4. *gamelan* orchestra; 5. *dalang*
80. Answers will vary. Sample answer: Because the flooding leaves behind a rich deposit of fertile soil, which is ideal for agriculture, and because the flooding is a natural way of irrigating the land. This regular flooding makes the land ideal for growing rice, the country's main source of food; Cambodia produces more than 2 million tons of rice each year.
81. Answers will vary. Students should refer to the many separate islands where people live, and the country's ethnic diversity (Malay, Papuan, Chinese, indigenous tribes) and linguistic variety (Bahasa Indonesia is the official language, but many local dialects are spoken, for a total of some 730 languages).

82. Answers will vary. Sample answer: The climate of Malaysia is sunny, hot, and humid. Stilt houses were suitable for this environment for several reasons. The stilts meant that all the house's exterior surfaces were exposed to any available breeze, increasing ventilation. The many windows and few interior partitions also furthered ventilation. The deep eaves shaded the walls from solar radiation and protected the interior from rain in the rainy season. The low thermal capacity of the building materials meant that the house did not retain heat.

83. Answers will vary. Sample answer: Mopeds are cheaper than cars; they are fuel-efficient; and they're so much smaller than cars that they are a good solution in densely populated areas.

84. 1. b; 2. c; 3. d; 4. e; 5. a; 6. d; 7. e; 8. e; 9. d; 10. a

85. Answers will vary. Sample answer: These proverbs show a strong connection with the ocean.

86. Answers will vary.

87. Answers will vary. Sample answer: Each of these three sites was one-third of the way around the globe from the next site. Each would be able to receive signals from the moon at a different period of time (with some overlap). This meant that, no matter what time of day or night the *Eagle* landed on the moon, one of the sites would be able to receive the signal.

88. Ayers Rock (Uluru)

89. Answers will vary. Sample answer: The land area of the Solomon Islands may be small, but it covers a wide area and is broken into many islands. The scattered nature of these islands would make languages diverge and develop differently.

90. Answers will vary. Sample answer: They dislike this term because it was imposed on them during the process of colonization and because, as a blanket term, it ignores the differences between peoples in different parts of Australia.

91. Answers will vary. The facilities included on the requirement list for Canberra included: Houses of Parliament; governor-general's residence; prime minister's residence; departmental offices; courts; churches; mint; national art gallery and library;

state house; printing office; government factories; university; technical colleges; city hall; post office; museum; central railway station; railway marshaling yards; military barracks; criminal and police courts; jail; hospitals; national theater; central power station; gasworks; markets; stadium; parks and gardens

92. 1. c; 2. e; 3. d; 4. f; 5. a; 6. g; 7. b

93. Answers will vary.

94. 1. blood-red air 2. lake hole 3. hole exploding 4. peak moving 5. peak burning. These are all volcanoes, part of the Pacific Ring of Fire.

95. Answers will vary. Sample answer: Australia is very dry; 70 percent of the country receives less than 20 inches of rain every year. The Eastern Highlands receive the most rainfall in the country; that is why most of Australia's large cities are located here. Overall, the inland areas are driest, with most rainfall in coastal areas. That is why Australia's other cities are also near the coast.

96. 1. b; 2. e; 3. e; 4. e; 5. e; 6. c; 7. a; 8. a; 9. a; 10. d

97. 1. d; 2. e; 3. c; 4. b; 5. d; 6. a; 7. b

98. Answers will vary. Sample answer: 1. People who talk a lot often don't know very much. 2. Even when you think you know how to do something, it can't hurt to make sure by asking someone else. 3. If you work hard, even a seemingly impossible goal can be achieved. 4. Be careful what you say, because you never know who may hear you. 5. The weak are often hurt by the actions of the strong. 6. No matter how desperate the situation is, there is always hope.

99. Answers will vary. Possible answers: no problem is beyond our ability to address; it's important to see the big picture and work for change.

100. good manners—2, 3, 6; bad manners—1, 4, 5

101. 1. f; 2. b; 3. e; 4. a; 5. d; 6. c

102. 1. *Chan*; 2. *Sensei*; 3. *San*; 4. *Kun*

103. Answers will vary. Sample answer: Manga are a cheap, easy way to amuse yourself. The combination of words and pictures can bring a reader into a scene in a way that words alone cannot. With their interesting angles and many panels for a single movement, they can convey

delicate nuances. For complex topics such as history, being able to "see" what is going on can help the reader understand things better.

104. Answers will vary. Sample answer: I'm over the moon; once in a blue moon; to moon about; to shoot for the moon; the moon is made of green cheese.

105. The only items not invented first in China are 10. photography, 12. refrigerator, 14. sewing machine, and 15. thermometer.

106. The Great Wall of China

107. Mount Fuji

108. Answers will vary. Sample answer: My first step would be to analyze the sounds that make English unique, and make sure I developed characters for those sounds.

109. 1. f; 2. d; 3. b; 4. a; 5. e; 6. c

110. 1. d; 2. e; 3. g; 4. h; 5. c; 6. a; 7. b; 8. f

111. 1. 1953; 2. 1948; 3. 1392; 4. 1910; 5. 1945; 6. 1292; 7. 2333 B.C.E.; 8. 1950

112. Answers will vary.

113. Answers will vary. Sample answer: Basho meant

that you can't really understand things by reading books about them or by talking to people; you have to look at the thing itself to understand it.

114. a. Chiang Kai-shek b. Zhou Enlai c. Mao Zedong d. Sun Yat-sen

115. 1. d; 2. a; 3. b; 4. e; 5. f; 6. c

116. 1. c; 2. e; 3. b; 4. a; 5. f; 6. d

117. Answers will vary. Sample answer: The moon is seen at a different angle, depending on the viewer's location. The same lunar features create different illusions in different places.

118. Answers will vary. Sample answer: In China, since cities are so densely populated, increased car ownership will create huge changes in cities, including increased congestion, pollution, traffic jams, parking problems, and more accidents between cars and bikes. Also, the move from an active form of transportation (bikes) to a passive form (cars) will have a negative effect on people's health. Globally, an increase in car ownership in China will lead to increased global pollution and greenhouse gases. With a population of more than

a billion, if China were to reach private ownership levels of even one car for every 10 people (the current global average, which includes developing nations), that would be 126 million cars, a huge increase. It would also mean a huge increase in per-person consumption of petroleum products. Currently, the average American consumes 23 barrels of oil a year; the average Chinese consumes $\frac{2}{3}$ of a barrel. Increasing Chinese oil consumption will mean a huge drain on global petroleum resources.

119.   1. a; 2. d; 3. b; 4. d; 5. e; 6. f; 7. e; 8. c

120.   Answers will vary. Sample answers: 1. Don't give advice to someone who knows more about a subject than you do. 2. If you plan to cause trouble for someone else, your bad deed will inevitably have negative consequences for you. 3. People should focus on their own projects and occupations, and not give advice about things they don't have training in. 4. You shouldn't spend more than you can afford. 5. Don't worry about unimportant things; don't exaggerate small problems.

121.   Answers will vary. Sample answer: You may be weak alone, but with others, you can withstand even a powerful enemy.

122.   Answers will vary. Problems include the fact that most adult Azerbaijanis are familiar only with the Cyrillic alphabet, which was in use for seventy years. Only a few, much older adults learned the Latin alphabet between 1928 and 1938. All printing presses, publishers, newspapers, and textbooks used Cyrillic. The transition was begun with Latin-alphabet textbooks for first-graders. Each year, the textbooks for the next grade level are printed in the Latin alphabet. Thus, students in older grades use textbooks printed in Cyrillic, while those in lower grades use only Latin. In 1992, TV stations began using the Latin alphabet for written material on their broadcasts, such as titles. In 1997, newspapers began to print presidential decrees and parliamentary news in Latin. More books are being published in Latin, though Cyrillic is still the primary alphabet of

publishing. Street signs, advertising, and such things as labels on canned food are increasingly being written in the Latin alphabet.

123. Answers will vary.

124. Answers will vary. Sample answer: If a mosquito had just had a meal before it was trapped, the blood could have DNA from the animal the mosquito dined on.

125. St. Basil's Cathedral

126. Count Leo Tolstoy

127. Answers will vary. Many students will realize that the Internet is today's version of *samizdat*, a *samizdat* that no government can truly control.

128. Note: You may want to explain to students that these words have been transliterated from Cyrillic script. 1. jazz; 2. jeans; 3. menu; 4. method; 5. office; 6. officer; 7. parachute; 8. pajamas; 9. theater; 10. cylinder; 11. jacket; 12. jury

129. 1. d; 2. c; 3. e; 4. b; 5. a

130. Answers will vary. Sample answer: Yeltsin was one of the architects of the breakup of the Soviet Union. His attempts to speed the pace of reform in the U.S.S.R. led to the collapse of the union.

Yeltsin hoped this would bring improvements to the lives of Russian residents. However, he wasn't so concerned with freedom for non-Russian members of the U.S.S.R.; in December 1994, he sent Russian troops into the Muslim minority region of Chechnya to put down a separatist rebellion.

131. Answers will vary. Sample answer: Vladimir Lenin, leader who overthrew the Russian government to found a Communist state; Joseph Stalin, Lenin's ruthless successor; Nikita Khrushchev, one of Stalin's top advisors and his successor; Leonid Brezhnev, president of the U.S.S.R. who led invasions of Czechoslovakia (1968) and Afghanistan (1977); Mikhail Gorbachev, president of the Soviet Union whose policies of *glasnost* and *perestroika* led to the dismantling of the U.S.S.R.; Boris Yeltsin, president of Russia after the collapse of the Soviet Union.

132. Note: You may want to tell students that *lubki* is the plural form of the word; *lubok* is the singular. Answers will vary. Sample answer: Cartoons

(especially political cartoons), comic books, and caricatures all share many of these characteristics: clear images, bright colors, often including captions, used to tell stories or make fun of political figures.

133. Answers will vary. Sample answer: Uzbekistan was the crossroads for trade caravan routes between the Middle East and both China and India. Arab merchants carried silk from China and spices from India, then sold them in Europe. Only in the fifteenth century, when European explorers found a sea route to China and India, did the importance of the Silk Route wane.

134. Answers will vary. Sample answer: Although Russia had an extensive coastline, all of Russia's ports were far from Europe. Most of them were so far north they could not be used during the winter. By gaining access to the Baltic Sea, Peter gained access to European trade, thus furthering his goal of making Russia a major European power.

135. Answers will vary. Student answers may include some of the following: climate modification effect has been lost—area is now hotter in summer, colder in winter, drier all year round; soil salinization; increased erosion; loss of wetlands around the lake means that the wetlands' pollution-filtering mechanism has been lost; shortage of drinking water; loss of water-based livelihoods, such as fishing; disappearance of other wildlife that depended on sea for water, food; reduction of food supply for people in the area.

136. Answers will vary.

137. 1. e; 2. d; 3. f; 4. b; 5. a; 6. c

138. Answers will vary.

139. Answers will vary. Sample answer: The Greeks believed that physical exercise and mental training were connected. Athletic competition was a way for a hero to demonstrate his virtue and gain renown for his city-state. Also, many of the events demonstrated an athlete's ability as a warrior. Wrestling, boxing, hurling the javelin, even running, were all skills required of a warrior in ancient times.

140. 1. c; 2. b; 3. e; 4. f; 5. d; 6. a

141. The Leaning Tower of Pisa
142. Dutch—cookie, cruise, easel; French—café, garage, regime; German—delicatessen, hamburger, kindergarten; Italian—confetti, piano, spaghetti; Spanish—canyon, guitar, mosquito
143. 1. Achilles' heel—a person's one incurable weakness; Achilles' tendon—the tendon that stretches from the heel bone to the calf muscle; 2. mentor—wise and trustworthy counselor or teacher; 3. odyssey—long, circuitous approach to reaching a goal; 4. siren song—something irresistible but dangerous.
144. Answer: Bosnia and Herzegovina; Croatia; Former Yugoslav Republic of Macedonia; Slovenia; Serbia and Montenegro
145. Margaret Thatcher
146. Gustav Mahler
147. 1. I; 2. N; 3. I; 4. N; 5. I; 6. N; 7. I; 8. I; 9. N; 10. I; 11. I; 12. I; 13. N; 14. N; 15. I; 16. N
148. *Note:* The versions of the words given in the box are simplified pronunciations; they do not show the way the words are actually written in Gaelic.

The actual words are *baile, carraig, dubh, linn,* and *mór.* However, they are pronounced as given in the box. 1. c; 2. a; 3. e; 4. f; 5. b; 6. d
149. Answers will vary. Sample answer: London is sited on a river valley, in a low-lying area. The river provides moisture for fog, and the low hills around the valley keep the fog from dispersing. Also, winds from the east bring pollution from industrial areas in continental Europe.
150. Answers will vary.
151. Answers will vary. Sample answer: Advantages would be not having to change money to go from one country to another, especially for businesses doing trade with other countries. Disadvantages would include something of a loss of national identity, especially for a country like Greece, which used the drachma as its currency for so long.
152. 1. L; 2. J; 3. L; 4. J; 5. J; 6. L; 7. L; 8. T; 9. T; 10. T; 11. F; 12. T
153. Answers will vary.
154. Answers will vary. Sample answer: The three

major components of Brazilian culture are the indigenous peoples of Brazil, Africans, and the Portuguese. *Capoeira* comes from a Tupi-Guarani word. It was created by enslaved Africans in protest against their treatment by the Portuguese.

155. Answers will vary. Many students will point out that Halloween, as celebrated in the United States, bears some resemblance to the Days of the Dead, with skeletons, sweets, and macabre decorations.

156. Answers will vary. Sample answer: The forests are being cut down by people who live in the forest and need land to grow crops, and—often illegally—by people who want to harvest the trees to sell. We could stop illegal lumber harvesting by setting up a system of certifying wood that does not come from the rain forest, and refusing to import wood that isn't certified. To stop clear-cutting of the forests for agriculture, we could support programs to teach people of the rain forest about sustainable agriculture.

157. The Galapagos Islands

158. Machu Picchu, Peru

159. Answers will vary, but students should note that the geography of the region promoted the development of distinct languages. The volcanic mountains of the north and dense rain forest of the south tended to keep groups separate from one another, facilitating separate linguistic development.

160. Answers will vary.

161. Answers will vary. Sample answer: Simón Bolívar—Venezuelan, nicknamed "the Liberator," who led many colonies to independence from Spain, including Venezuela, Colombia, Panama, Bolivia, and Ecuador; Miguel Hidalgo—a Catholic priest who led the fight against the Spanish government in Mexico. In a speech in 1810, he called on Mexicans to fight for independence and liberty. Hidalgo was captured and executed. Mexico declared independence in 1821; Bernardo O'Higgins—Irish-Chilean landowner who helped bring about Chilean independence; José de San Martín—Argentinean who helped Chile and Peru

to independence; François Toussaint-Louverture—former slave who led a revolution in Haiti. Captured by French officers, he was imprisoned in France, where he died in 1803. In 1804 the rebels defeated the French army, and Haiti proclaimed its independence.

162. Answers will vary.

163. Fidel Castro

164. Answers will vary.

165. Answers will vary. Sample answer: Amazon Basin rain forest—heavy rains encourage dense vegetation, remarkable biological diversity; heat, rain, and insects make the area hard to live in, and the thin soil makes agriculture difficult. La Pampas—fertile plain with plentiful rainfall, used for farming, raising livestock.

166. Answers will vary. Sample answer: The Yanomamo have learned a lot from Western culture, but they don't think people in the West have learned anything from them, even though there were things in their culture that could have benefited other people.

167. Answers will vary. Sample answer: honesty, punctuality, industry, education, courtesy.

168. Answers will vary.

169. 1. b; 2. c; 3. a

170. The Grand Canyon

171. L'Anse aux Meadows, Newfoundland

172. 1. cyborg (cybernetic + organism); 2. sitcom (situation + comedy); 3. brunch (breakfast + lunch); 4. guesstimate (guess + estimate); 5. motel (motor + hotel); 6. stagflation (stagnation + inflation)

173. a. 1; b. 7; c. 9; d. 8; e. 11; f. 2; g. 10; h. 3; i. 5; j. 4; k. 6; l. 9

174. 1. John Adams; 2. Samuel Adams; 3. Benjamin Franklin; 4. John Hancock; 5. Patrick Henry; 6. Thomas Jefferson; 7. James Otis; 8. Thomas Paine; 9. Paul Revere; 10. George Washington

175. 1. L; 2. A; 3. L; 4. A; 5. S; 6. L; 7. M; 8. L; 9. S; 10. M; 11. M; 12. S; 13. S; 14. A; 15. A ; 16. M

176. 1. trumpet; 2. cornet; 3.tenor sax; 4. trumpet; 5. piano; 6. voice; 7. trumpet; 8. voice

177. Answers will vary. Some major national parks and

monuments: Parks: Acadia, Maine; Badlands, South Dakota; Death Valley, California and Nevada; Denali, Arkansas; Everglades, Florida; Glacier Bay, Alaska; Grand Canyon, Arizona; Grand Teton, Wyoming; Great Smoky Mountains, North Carolina and Tennessee; Haleakala, Hawaii; Hot Springs, Arkansas; Mesa Verde, Colorado; Mount Rainier, Washington; Sequoia, California; Yellowstone, Wyoming, Montana, and Idaho; Yosemite, California; Zion, Utah; Monuments: Canyon de Chelly, Arizona; Carlsbad Caverns, New Mexico; Chaco Canyon, New Mexico; Mount Rushmore, South Dakota

178. Answers will vary.
179. The car. Wartime restrictions during WWII left many Americans with extra money—money they had been unable to use while goods were unavailable. Mass production made cars more available, and many Americans soon found that cars narrowed the gap between urban and rural life. The development of a national interstate highway system in the 1950s and 1960s increased mobility and encouraged businesses to move outward to sites where land is cheaper and access by car and truck is easier than in cities.

180. Answers will vary. Student answers should include such concepts as "I feel . . . [sore, well, in pain]," "I want [a tissue, a blanket, to use the telephone]," "I cannot [breathe, walk, move my arms]," "I feel faint," and so forth.

Turn downtime into learning time!

Other books in the
Daily *Warm-Ups* series:

- Algebra
- Algebra II
- Analogies
- Biology
- Character Education
- Chemistry
- Commonly Confused Words
- Critical Thinking
- Earth Science
- Geography
- Geometry
- Journal Writing
- Mythology

- Physics
- Poetry
- Pre-Algebra
- Prefixes, Suffixes, & Roots
- Shakespeare
- Spelling & Grammar
- Test-Prep Words
- U.S. History
- Vocabulary
- World History
- World Religions
- Writing